# Ghost Waters

## Canada's

## Haunted Seas and Shores

## Darryll Walsh

Pottersfield Press, Lawrencetown Beach, Nova Scotia,
Canada

© Copyright Darryll Walsh 2002

All rights reserved. No part of this publication may be reproduced or transmitted in any form or by any means, electronic or mechanical, including photocopying, or by any information storage or retrieval system, without permission in writing from the publisher.

**National Library of Canada Cataloguing in Publication**

Walsh, Darryll
Ghost waters: Canada's haunted seas and shores

ISBN 1-895900-49-2

1. Apparitions – Canada. 2. Haunted places – Canada. 3. Curiosities
and wonders – Canada. I. Title.
GR113.W34 2002          133.1'0971          C2002-902850-7


**Book cover design by Dalhousie Graphics with photo files from
Art Cosgrove and Lesley Choyce
Maps by Art Cosgrove**


Pottersfield Press acknowledges the ongoing support of the Nova Scotia Department of Tourism and Culture, Cultural Affairs Division. We acknowledge the support of the Canada Council for the Arts which last year invested $19.1 million in writing and publishing throughout Canada. We also acknowledge the finanacial support of the Government of Canada through the Book Publishing Industry Development Program for our publishing activities.


Pottersfield Press
83 Leslie Road
East Lawrencetown, Nova Scotia, Canada B2Z 1P8
Web site: www.pottersfieldpress.com
To order, phone 1-800-NIMBUS9 (1-800-646-2879)
Printed in Canada

Canada Council
for the Arts
Conseil des Arts
du Canada
Canada

NOVASCOTIA
Tourism and Culture

# Dedication

We often don't realize the effect we have on others, both good and bad. Sometimes it goes unseen and seemingly unnoticed, yet a brief moment in time can last for an eternity. I dedicate this book to those special people who have touched my life for the better, and likely have no knowledge of having done so. Through your encouragement, friendship, love, or favour you have brightened my life and I do remember you.

# Acknowledgements

Every writing project is dependent on the help of others. All writers become whoever they are because of the assistance and work of the unsung heroes who help in the research, editing and publishing of their work. To that end I owe a large thank you to my publisher Lesley Choyce and the editor of this work, Julia Swan. I must also thank Peter Coade from ATV for his gracious assistance, Art Cosgrove for supplying the maps, and Sherry Yates for her help in putting the manuscript together. And of course I must thank my parents, family, and friends for their love and support.

PACIFIC
OCEAN

HUDSON
BAY

ATLANTIC
OCEAN

UNITED STATES OF AMERICA

5
3
4
2

1. Lake Ontario
2. Lake Erie
3. Lake Huron
4. Lake Michigan
5. Lake Superior

# Contents

# Introduction

As a parapsychologist and writer I am most commonly asked two questions. Firstly, why did you become a parapsychologist, and secondly, what in the paranormal do you believe is real?

Of the two questions, the first is much easier to answer. Because of my family and cultural history I have abandoned the safe environs of academia and psychological practice to chase after mysteries that many consider irrelevant. As I grew up my family often visited my mother's childhood home in River Bourgeois, Cape Breton. My grandmother and Uncle Al lived there and I spent many a wonderful and serene hour playing on that hill overlooking the river. As the inevitable hour of our departure for Halifax approached, my uncle would come to me and offer to give me one of his books on World War II history or on ghosts. He had been in the RCAF during the Second World War and naturally had an interest in the conflict. The reason for his interest in ghosts I did not find out about until after his death in 1998. Consequently, as a result of all these books, by the time I was a teenager I had compiled a fair amount of knowledge on both subjects. Although I set out to become a psychologist, it isn't much of a surprise to me that my life took a little detour on the way to the couch.

Even though I have been intensely interested in the para-normal since childhood, and have devoured every fictional or non-fictional book and movie, my family must not have known how seriously interested I was. It was only in the fall of 2000 upon the release of my first book, *Ghosts of Nova Scotia*, that the family history of hauntings came out. I finally found out that the house I grew up in on Edgewood Avenue and the house in River Bourgeois were haunted. Shortly before his death, my mother asked Uncle Al if he ever went upstairs (where I slept quite peacefully as a child) and he replied there were too many ghosts up there for him. On top of that, my mother finally told me she used to see or hear someone walking in the downstairs hall and strange knocking sounds were heard in the TV room. But I grew up blissfully unaware of all this, and I still think I could walk through most ghosts without seeing them. I do not have the knack. But I am hopeful.

Three feet from my bed sits the rocking chair from River Bourgeois that rocked for four days in 1945 prior to my mother's hearing of Uncle Augustine's death in Holland. Neither my Uncles Augustine or Al nor my beloved grandmother has decided to pay me a visit, though they have an open invitation. But as I said before, they could have been there, or there now, and I probably wouldn't see them.

As for what I believe in, I would have to say I believe in the search. I believe that any mystery should be investigated, and if true, added to our knowledge, and if false, purged from our consideration. There would be some great philosophical and/or theological implications should some areas of the paranormal be confirmed. But most lay down the road for when the level of detection becomes more precise and we can measure the changes to the environment that must occur when a paranormal event happens. At that time, some of these mysteries will no longer be paranormal, but science. If someone should find Sasquatch, or Ogopogo, then it will move from cryptozoology to zoology in a heartbeat. The paranormal is only something we do not understand or classify yet. We may never truly understand what a "near-death experience" is. Most of what occurs happens on the "other" side of life. We have a better chance at determining the true nature of a ghost once the equipment is ready. I am most hopeful in the area of ghosts and it is the concept that I most believe in.

Other phenomena, such as the Bermuda Triangle or Atlantis, we can readily classify as a hoax in the first case and a boring archaeological search in the second. The Bermuda Triangle is easily quantifiable. Are there more ships and planes disappearing in this body of water than elsewhere? No, there are not. Simple number crunching. What is the nature of Atlantis? Just another civilization that flourished and died many thousands of years ago should Plato be literal in his description. No fantastic energies, or alien races, or any of the other garbage we humans have created in our minds to amuse ourselves and the gullible. These are easy to understand.

The next level of mysteries are those that are a little less quantifiable, but we can guess at their likely nature. Alien abduction is almost certainly the result of a misuse of hypnosis (which should never be used in the paranormal), and easily understood and common sleep disorders. Before aliens we saw fairies, and before them we saw demons and witches, in the same circumstances, either waking up, or falling asleep. As our beliefs changed, so did our goblins. The only added aspect is hypnosis, which some use to buttress their belief systems. Hypnosis is a state of heightened suggestibility used for the treatment of some common disorders and relief of pain. You cannot use a clinical intervention whose nature is heightened suggestibility and imagination to determine truth.

There is a tendency to think that if you believe in one aspect of the paranormal you must believe in all of the paranormal. Or that there is some unifying force that connects each mystery together. There isn't. They are all separate and should be investigated with that in mind. A psychic would no more be able to speak with the dead than a medium would be able to dowse for water or gold.

Some people wonder why, if I am so careful in my research into the nature of the paranormal, I write stories that are probably mostly fiction. They miss the point. None of us is or should be a captive of one dimension. I am quite able to take off my scientist's hat and become that ten-year-old boy who eagerly took the offered book from his uncle. I am still that child who would crawl out to the now notorious hallway and listen carefully to his parents talk to visitors and hope they would bring up the rocking chair story again. Goosebumps demand no proof, only possibilities. (For more information on my scientific search and how to contact me, see pages 138-140.)

Unlike the paranormal, the stories in this book are connected by the unifying motif of water. It has been the instrument of our discovery, exploration, and development. It was the original superhighway and it has nourished us for centuries. It is our most precious resource and the one most taken for granted. But it also the one which has spawned the most eerie and mysterious of stories. I do not present them as fact. I do not know their true nature. I only know the tingle they give as I type them. Now is not the time to understand these mysteries, but to marvel at their possibilities .

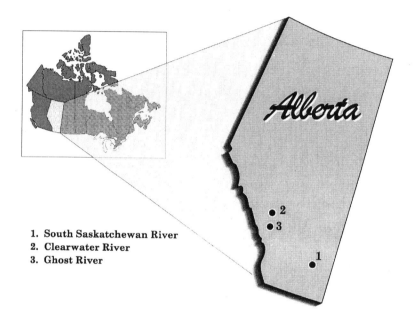

1. South Saskatchewan River
2. Clearwater River
3. Ghost River

# Alberta

There are a few lakes and rivers in Alberta that claim mysterious creatures inhabiting them, but details are scarce and almost unknown to anyone outside the immediate locality.

## South Saskatchewan River

Since 1949 there have been numerous reports of a creature that has instilled fear in local residents. Commonly reported as being three to four metres in length, serpentine and darkly coloured, the creature has frightened locals enough that the army reserve has been called in to guard residents and their property. Chances are this creature is more likely a snake or eel and that people's imaginations or viewing factors have greatly added to its reputation. But whatever the reason for the sightings the fear is palpable to those who believe.

# Clearwater River

A far more dangerous beast is reported in this river, especially near Rocky Mountain House. The beast is described as being more than six metres long with red eyes, and is dark gray in colour. It also has a liking for beef, for it has been observed grabbing a small calf on the riverbank and taking its prize to a watery doom.

# Ghost River

The name Ghost River may conjure up a sense of romance or delightful excitement, but this river is aptly named. There are not just one or two ghosts said to be seen on or around the river, but dozens, perhaps hundreds!

Ghost River is a part of the Ghost River Wilderness Area, which is just outside of Banff National Park and north of Canmore. The Stoney Indians used the riverbanks as burial sites for many years. Also, in 1870 a great number of natives died when they were cut down by an unknown illness. Soon afterwards, smallpox decimated a third of the population and many natives and explorers reported seeing the haunting apparitions of sick and dying natives along the banks of the river. It was even said that ghostly bands of natives, some on horseback, others running on foot, were seen hunting buffalo. The area was avoided for years, and the place where most natives died is now covered by the site of the very aptly named Ghost Dam. No one is sure of the true number of phantoms that haunt this land but the legend of the river of death and its countless spirits lives on.

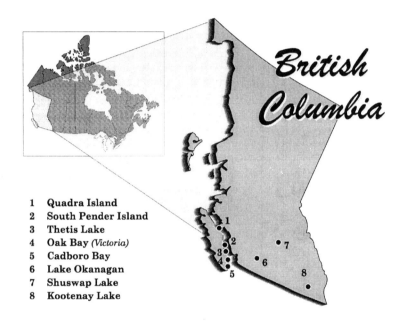

1   Quadra Island
2   South Pender Island
3   Thetis Lake
4   Oak Bay *(Victoria)*
5   Cadboro Bay
6   Lake Okanagan
7   Shuswap Lake
8   Kootenay Lake

# British Columbia

## The Pugwis

North America's West Coast legends of nasty humanoid creatures are similar to those of their Atlantic cousins. In BC they are called the Pugwis and are described as horrible looking men who bear a passing resemblance to the Creature From the Black Lagoon. Fish-faced with long fangs, these creatures lurk the long BC coastline looking for prey.

## Megladon

Unlike many cryptozoological animals said to inhabit our waterways, Megladon actually existed during the Miocene and Pliocene epochs, roughly 25 million to 1.6 million

17

years ago. Megladon (*Carcharodon megladon*) is the name given to a gigantic shark that prowled the depths of the world's oceans, and is regarded by some as the precursor of today's Great White Shark (*Carcharadon carcharias*). On average it grew to be twelve metres long, but longer lengths were probably attained. Some scientists believe it is possible for some species of large sharks (in excess of fifteen metres) to exist deep within today's oceans, so a relic like Megladon is possible, if unlikely. Megladon probably snacked upon whales and, if they were scarce, perhaps the odd shark or two. Its mouth could reportedly open to two metres in diameter, which is more than enough to swallow whole many sea creatures or you and me.

Reports have come from the BC coast of incredibly large sharks, fifteem to thirty metres long, prowling the coast looking for prey; in 1918 fishermen off Australia reported being accosted by a 35-metre shark that ate their catch and fishing equipment. A similar creature has also been reported off the California coast around San Francisco. Although rarely seen off British Columbia it is important to remember that sharks exist in every sea in the world, even the Arctic Ocean.

# South Pender Island

The Strait of Georgia separates Vancouver Island from the mainland of British Columbia and the state of Washington in the United States. Among the many islands in this strait is South Pender Island, and stories are told of a creature that prowls the waters around the island. It is said to have a long serpentine body with a horse-like head with no ears or nose.

Unlike other sea serpents, this one is described as having a long, dark brown stripe running along the length of a grayish-brown body on both sides. The 12-metre-long creature has been rarely seen, which may indicate it is nomadic, unlike the Cadborasaurus or Megladon, which appears territorial. If one searches zoological records for a possible creature that fits the bill, then the ancient Zeuglodon (whale), which existed at the same time as Megladon, would probably be the closest match. Since Megladon probably snacked on Zeuglodons, perhaps this is why the South Pender Island creature is so rarely sighted. Why stick around and become dinner?

Besides the sea serpent seen off the coast of this island, South Pender is also well known for the resort haunted by the ghost of a native woman murdered in the nineteenth century.

The history of Canada makes little mention of the Spanish who made their way up the Pacific coast of North America before the English either crossed over the Rockies from landward or sailed up the coast themselves. The Spanish were the first explorers to reach much of the coast of British Columbia, and this included South Pender Island in 1791. South Pender Island has fresh water springs, which were a godsend to ships that were far from home and needed replenishment.

The Spanish were gone by the 1800s, though, when a young native girl was brutally raped and murdered by two European men. She had been minding her own business, digging for clams on the beach, when these two murderers decided to have their way with her, then beat her to death with a pair of oars by a yew tree. It is said the oars are still visible to this day with the yew tree grown up around them. It is near here that the pitiful vision of the native girl is seen wandering through the woods, as well as above the resort on a hill. It has also been reported that her ghost can be seen sometimes in the apartments of the resort employees and the Bedwell Harbour Island Pub. Once a painting of the area of the murder scene was put up in the pub and the picture refused to stay on the wall. When the painting was replaced with another, the problem ceased.

The spirit of the poor murdered girl is not the only ghost on the island. At one time there was a great battle among native tribes located where the Indian Reserve is now. Many men lost their lives and it is said that the apparition of one particular warrior, tall and dark, can be seen from time to time on the reserve.

# Cadboro Bay

Cadboro Bay lies just outside of the capital city, Victoria, on Vancouver Island. From this picturesque bay come reports of a serpentine monster, twenty-four to thirty metres long. It is reported to have a horse-like head with whiskers around its large mouth. Along its back it is said to have a dorsal crest or mane, with an overall colour of dark gray, brown or black. The eyes are described as being black and bulbous, which shine red or green. The creature has long, shark-like teeth and two large fangs.

Even with this fierce description, Cadborosaurus or Caddy, as the creature has been named, is deemed to be harmless and doesn't strike fear in the local residents. The citizens of the area had a name-the-monster contest and Caddy was the winning entry. It has remained a favourite pet ever since.

Unlike similar creatures from many lakes, Caddy has a wider assortment of possible foods. It has been seen eating sea plants, fish and the odd bird that strayed too close for its own good. There have also been reports of a second monster, slightly smaller, which some believe to be Caddy's mate. And in 1968, a much smaller monster was sighted and presumed to be a baby Caddy. They are said to swim as one would expect worms to, although their bodies are as wide as an automobile. There have been more than five hundred reported sightings of Caddy.

In 1937 the corpse of a creature many believe was a Cadborasaurus was recovered from a sperm whale's stomach. It was three metres long and had the horse-like head and serpentine body so often reported by witnesses to Caddy. A picture was taken of the corpse, but the body was soon lost. Although proof of Caddy may be lost, the creature sure isn't. He was regularly sighted during the 1990s.

# Roberts Creek

Another interesting creature coming to us from the Strait of Georgia is described as similar to Cadborasaurus. Roberts Creek is just northwest of Vancouver, across from Victoria, so some believe this creature may be Caddy or a relative.

Reports from 1932 described a long serpentine creature with a horse-like head. Unlike the South Pender Island beast, though, this one had nostrils and either horns or ears sticking out of the sides of its head. There also appeared to be a small mane on top of the head that ran a very short way down the body. But like the South Pender Island creature, sightings of this monster are rare.

British Columbia probably has the most haunted lakes in Canada, followed closely by Quebec and Nova Scotia. Most of the stories are short with few details, or known only to local residents, but a few are world famous.

# Lake Okanagan

Lake Okanagan is a cold, deep, and large lake in the interior of British Columbia. The lake connects the Okanagan River with the Columbia, and the cities of Vernon, Penticton, and Kelowna are the main population centres closest to the lake. The lake is 127 kilometres long, one to three kilometres wide, and averages seventy-six metres deep with a maximum depth of 245 metres. The temperature is maintained at a cool 1°C year round.

Another year-round aspect to this lake is its number one resident, Ogopogo, the most famous lake monster in all of Canada. It was known as N'ha-a-tik or Na-ha-ha-itk to the Shuswap and Okanakane natives and had a reputation as a fearsome and deadly creature. It was thought to reside in a cave at Squally Point and when natives crossed the lake they would bring small animals to throw in the water as a sacrifice to the creature. There is even a story of bones, blood and fat seen strewn along the shore of an island forty kilometres from Penticton. The creature was most often seen between this island and Mission Valley.

In the 1860s the first European settlers began to see this creature and described it as twenty-two metres long, serpentine, with a sheep- or horse-like head, blunt nose, whiskers, and a fin running from its head down the length of its body. The body itself was said to have dark coloured centimetre-wide scales. It had four flippers, a forked tongue and there is even an odd story of flipper prints being seen on land once.

This description of the creature hasn't really changed in the intervening years, but the reputation of Ogopogo sure has. The natives always feared it and were constantly on their guard when on the lake. The Europeans, however, first viewed the creature as a mystery then as a pet or mascot as the years went by. Today, Ogopogo is a big attraction in the tourist sweepstakes for the area. The city of Kelowna has even made Ogopogo an honorary citizen.

The attraction of Ogopogo increased immensely when two alleged films of the creature were taken in 1968 and 1976. In 1968 Art Folden took a 55-second film of something moving snake-like through the water. Although indistinct, the film proved interesting to local residents. In 1976 Edward Fletcher was in a boat on the lake and about fifteen feet away when he shot his film of the creature. This film is a little clearer than the first one, but still not indisputable proof. The length of the creature was estimated to be twenty-two metres in the Fletcher film.

## Thetis Lake

Another strange creature is said to inhabit Thetis Lake near Victoria. The monster, first reported in the early 1970s, is said to be silver in colour, covered with scales, and has a fin that is located at the back of the skull. Its ears, hands, and feet are webbed, and its eyes are black and bulbous like a fly's. It is an amphibian since it has been seen on land as well as in the water.

## Shuswap Lake

This denizen of the deep is known by many names. Shuswaggi and Shoosy are just two for this brown coloured, multi-humped creature. The humps are said to rise thrity to sixty centimetres out of the water, and the creature casts a strong wake behind it as it races across the lake. The smallness of the humps would seem to suggest a more mundane animal rather than any cryptozoological specimen, and precise details of this mystery are few.

## Kootenay Lake

There are many more details concerning the mysterious beast that is said to haunt this lake, which is located 177 kilometres east of Lake Okanagan. The first two reports of this creature terrified local residents and resulted in armed guards being posted around the lake.

The first report came in 1900 from a ship captain, W.J. Kane, in command of the steamer *Marion*. He watched a four-metre animal swimming in the lake with prominent fins at the front of the body. At about the same time, a 12-year-old boy saw "a something" crawl out of the lake and snack on some debris washed up on the shore. Later investigation would reveal that this "something" was equipped with large webbed feet, and the thought of something large and unknown crawling ashore to feed was enough to have regular patrols established.

The creature described by the boy and others soon after resembled an alligator, of all animals. They reported a reptilian creature with scaly skin and short, stumpy legs. The jaws of the animal were said to look quite "vicious." The final report of that year actually stated the creature to be an alligator. As most readers will already know, Canadian lakes are too cold normally to permit a reptile like an alligator or Cayman. But the descriptions do fit this creature, and I suppose it is possible that someone, perhaps connected with a circus, decided to leave one of their attractions behind as they passed through the area. A little detective work rummaging around old newspapers might be in order here.

The next sighting of the creature came in 1937, as it passed underneath a stalled sailboat, when it was described as being over seven metres long, dark, and with one hump. Its eyes were black and shiny and its mouth, unlike the earlier reports, was described as being small. Other unconfirmed reports came to light around that time, but nothing definite to give us a better idea of the nature of this anomaly.

## Quadra Island

One of the more interesting stories to come out of BC in the past few years has been that of the haunted doll in the Quesnel and District Museum in Quesnel. This doll, named Mandy (from the original Mereanda), reminds some people of the evil doll Chucky from the series of movies in the 1990s. Mandy is also said to be quite ugly and frightful and does not like to be moved or photographed. In fact, she seems to curse the equipment since cameras, camcorders, film or cassettes break or fail when around her. This eerie effect has a long history ever since the doll was manufactured somewhere in Germany in the 1920s.

The doll has been trouble for the two previous owners prior to the museum. They reported that the doll would make crying sounds, though she is incapable of making sounds. She moves around under her own power, disturbs rooms, opens windows and makes everyone who comes in contact with her uneasy. Perhaps her evil nature comes from the fact she has a large crack in her face that makes her right eye appear to be leering at those who look at her. Even dolls can be vain, perhaps?

## Oak Bay

Overlooking the Strait of Georgia in Victoria is the Victoria Golf Course at Oak Bay. In the 1930s a tragic story of murder and love played itself out in this beautiful location. It was the spring of 1936 when a loutish husband learned that his wife planned to divorce him due to his alcoholism and abusive nature. He murdered her by strangulation on the eighth hole and then in a momentary state of lucidity and regret, threw himself off the cliff and into the bay. The poor woman's spirit must be experiencing some misplaced sense of guilt because since her death the phantom of a lone woman can be seen on the edge of the cliff looking forlornly at the water below. She is described as being gray and misty and, though she is seen to be alone on that cliff, the sounds of other spirits can clearly be heard as well. Ghostly voices can be heard along the shoreline of the bay near the golf course and on rare occasions it is said that the locals have witnessed other misty forms near the gray lady. Local legend has it that every spring the phantom woman appears and the voices can be heard as if something in death draws this group of unfortunate souls back to the land of the living, if only for a short time.

1 Lake Winnipeg
2 Lake Winnipegosis
3 Lake Manitoba

# Manitoba

## Manitoba Lake System

Manitoba has a vast inland water system of rivers and lakes. Three lakes in particular, Lake Manitoba, Lake Winnipeg, and Lake Winnipegosis, as well as the Dauphin River, are said to be the home of a lake monster by the name of Manipogo.

Manipogo is often called the loudest Canadian lake monster due to its wide range of vocalizations. It has been heard to emit whistles, cries, laughs and even whispers. This should mean it is as well known as British Columbia's Ogopogo or Quebec's Champ, but the opposite is the case. Manipogo is often overlooked by cryptozoologists.

As with many lake monsters, Manipogo has a long history in Native mythology, but unlike most lake monsters, Manipogo's reputation is more of mystery than fear. The monster's noises have long been its hallmark, and the variety of its sounds have mystified and entranced observers for years. The Assiniboine called Lake Manitoba after the spirit they believed resided in the lake, the Manitou. Icelandic settlers called the creature Skirmski and noted its thundering and rumbling vibrations.

Manipogo is described as having the usual serpentine features with an overall length estimated to be twelve to eighteen metres. It is often compared to a large eel and is said to have a long horn on its flat head. Its body is reported to be smooth and dark in colour, and its range is huge. The combined surface area of its domain exceeds 33,000 square kilometres. More than enough room for a healthy family of reptilian creatures to live. And while Manitoba has some of the coldest weather in the country, except for the Arctic, this doesn't appear to bother Manipogo much, though it is said to be less active during winter.

1 Grand Falls
2 Lake Utopia
3 Miscou Island
4 Baie de Chaleur
5 Grand Manan Island
6 St Martins
7 Dungarvon River

# New Brunswick

## Baie des Chaleurs

The Baie des Chaleurs is the home of two marine oddities. The first is known and feared as the Gougou, a gigantic monster that Samuel de Champlain first heard about when he was exploring the region in 1603. Although he speaks of the monster as a male, popular belief is that it is a devil woman fifteen metres high. The body of the creature is covered with black scales and it has long green hair that looks like seaweed. The Gougou also has horrible yellow eyes, pointed ears and hideous fangs, topped off by huge claws for hands and large fins on her shoulders. Perhaps the most terrifying thing about the legend is her kangaroo-like pouch in which she stores her victims.

The other story from the rough waters of the Baie des Chaleurs is that of the more traditional ghost ship. This ship has been called the Fire Ship, the Burning Ship, the Phantom Ship, or the John Craig Light. No one knows for certain which vessel it is, or why it comes to us through the mists of time, but many along the Baie can recall their first sighting of it. The Fire Ship is reported primarily in late winter and summer and said to herald hurricanes and other major storms. There is a good possibility that there may be two completely different boats, since the John Craig Light is often described as just a glowing light swaying back and forth, as if a lantern were swinging from a mast. The Fire Ship is alternatively reported as a full-rigged boat with flames consuming the masts and phantom sailors running madly about the deck.

Although the Fire Ship may have been a vessel that was wrecked in the 1700s with few survivors, the favourite candidate is a French ship from the Battle of the Restigouche in 1760. This was the final naval battle of the Seven Years War between England and France, and the superior English fleet destroyed any chance the French had of continuing to control the waters of the Gulf of St. Lawrence. It is believed by some that the ship was actually a French ship manned by English sailors who had been captured earlier. Almost all eventually escaped, but six stayed behind to get into the rum carried in the ship's hold. The ship was set alight, but the six were too drunk to save themselves and perished. Is this the ship condemned to forever sail the bay, re-enacting its final moments? Or is it the ship that was beached at Green Point during a storm in the 1600s?

# Grand Falls

Few people realize that the St. John River is one of the longest rivers in the country. For much of its length it runs along the New Brunswick–Maine border, eventually emptying into the Bay of Fundy. Grand Falls is the name of both the town on the St. John River as well as the 23-metre waterfall nearby. Local legend has it that a brave woman by the name of Malabeam was captured by a war party of Mohawks and forced to lead them to the main camp of Maliseets from whence she came. Instead of leading them to her camp, she tricked the Mohawks and led them over the falls instead. To this day it is reported that you can hear her cries over the roar of the falls.

# The Nagumwasuck

The Irish are not the only race to have legends of the "little people," for many Native tribes along the Atlantic coast have similar legends of their own. The Nagumwasuck are one such legend in the provinces of New Brunswick and Nova Scotia and the state of Maine. They are said to be an exceptionally short and ugly people. Their height is about five centimetres and their thin bodies are covered with warts and boils. They are so thin in fact that if they wish to hide from humans, they just turn sideways and disappear! Their faces are thin and pointed, with black eyes that would seem to herald evil, but the Nagumwasuck are a peaceful people. Also known as the Wanagemeswak, these little people were hunted by the first European settlers so they are now shy and retiring, but they may make themselves known to people they regard as safe. A sighting of a Nagumwasuck is said to be very lucky!

## The Phantom Ship of Northumberland Strait

The Northumberland Strait is a body of water that runs between Prince Edward Island, New Brunswick, and Nova Scotia. It is 209 kilometres long and twelve to forty-eight kilometres wide. It can be very rough at times, or as still as a millpond. Winter is not a good time to ply the waters of the Strait. However, one ship is never in fear of the weather there.

No one is sure of the identity of the ghost ship, but first reports of it came out of Pictou in Nova Scotia in 1880. One night a three-masted ship was seen afire outside the harbour. Rescuers set out to help but the ship disappeared before their eyes. Since then people haven't approached the ship but have watched as it sails by. One interesting element of the mystery is that the ship always sails eastward and never in any other direction. Sometimes people are seen on the deck and at other times the decks are devoid of "life." The ship also varies its stay, some-times lasting for an hour, other times only lasting a few minutes. Of all the ghost ships in this book, The Phantom Ship of Northumberland Strait covers the most ground whether it stays for an hour or only a few minutes. Below is a chart of the places that frequently report sightings of the Phantom Ship of Northumberlabd Strait.

| New Brunswick | Nova Scotia | PEI |
|---|---|---|
| Richibucto | Wallace | Tignish |
| Buctouche | Pugwash | Summerside |
| Shediac | Mulgrave | Charlottetown |
| Baie Verte | Inverness | Murray Harbour |
| Tormentine | Cheticamp | Wood Islands |

# Grand Manan Island

In one American book Grand Manan Island is called the most haunted island in Canada, and while that may be hot-ly debated by other candidates for the honour, Grand Manan certainly has its share of eerie stories.

There are said to be at least five ghosts haunting this beautiful island. Some of the place names reflect these eerie legends — Ghost Hollow, Dark Harbour, and Little Dark Harbour cast a spell of mystery and suspense over the island.

At Ghost Hollow is the spectre of the Little Man who chases automobiles on foggy nights. He wears dark clothes and a flat-topped hat and throws himself in front of cars, terrifying unsuspecting motorists.

Along the coast of the island, about three kilometres from Dark Harbour, is the headless ghost of a man who was hanged when he and his wife were caught watching pirates burying their treasure. He roams the area looking for his wife, Desilda, who also haunts the area while screaming his name. She had survived the horrifying ordeal but died alone and insane on the island.

At Little Dark Harbour is the ghost of the Rowing Man. He appears during the full moon in November, silently paddling along in his ghostly canoe. If you're brave enough and listen carefully as he goes by, you may hear the splashing of the oars as they propel the phantom canoe and rower past you.

The last ghost is that of a Native woman, a Passmaquoddy maiden who is seen at Indian Beach every seven years. She is known as the Flaming Indian Woman because she stands quietly at the beach for a time before flames begin to consume her and eventually her body is burned to ashes, which the sea carries away. The only sound made during all this is that of a strange gurgling as she is reduced to dust.

# Miscou Island

From the waters around Miscou Island come ancient stories of a feminine creature known to instill the deepest terror in the hearts of those who sailed the Baie des Chaleurs. When Samuel de Champlain first charted these waters the local natives warned him of the loud hissing monster that inhabited a cave along the shore of Miscou Island. The creature was said to stand fifteen metres high and have black scales covering her repulsive body. Her hair had the look of seaweed and was of a dark green colour. Her yellow eyes pierced the night and she was also equipped with long sharp fangs to help devour unsuspecting sailors. Incredibly, she was said to have a pouch such as marsupials have in which to store her next meal. Mercifully, the victims would drown once she submerged so they would not have to endure the stark terror of being eaten alive.

Miscou Island lies between the Baie des Chaleurs and the Northumberland Strait and shares their stories of phantom ships. It is said that Miscou Island has its own phantom ship dating from the beginning of the nineteenth century. Legend states that the vicious Captain Craig, a well-known pirate of those days, preyed upon native settlements. It was this predatory nature that would lead to his ruin. A pilot he hired to guide him through the treacherous waters discovered and freed two captive native girls the captain and his crew were keeping below decks for some nefarious purposes. Shortly afterward the ship ran aground on Misocu Rock and everyone but the pilot drowned. Since that time, a red light can be seen to come out of Miscou Rock and gradually turn into the pirate ship. The ship glides across the bay, fully afire, until it reaches a sandbar where it abruptly extinguishes. Some say it presages tragedy, and can be seen day or night, all year long.

## Lake Utopia

Lake Utopia is near St. George in southern New Brunswick and boasts one of the more famous lake monsters in Atlantic Canada. The lake itself, however, is small, too small to support a monster of any great size one would think, yet stories abound of a 30-metre creature terrorizing those foolish enough to venture on the lake. It is described as a "terrible, voracious serpent" and that "blood drips constantly from the monster's mouth." Even in winter it is said the creature can reach up through the ice and grab its hapless victims, pulling them to their doom. In summer, boaters and swimmers also have to face the threat of the junk the creature dislodges from the bottom as it travels to and from its lair. Old canoes, logs, trees, and other debris have been known to suddenly rise to the surface, causing damage to boats and frightening swimmers. Of all the lake monsters in Canada the Lake Utopia Monster has kept its fierce reputation.

# St. Martins

The Maritimes certainly have the greatest concentration of ghost ships anywhere in the world, and from St. Martins comes the story of another ghostly ship of flames seen regularly every fall. During the months of September and October lucky persons can catch sight of the three-master as it slowly makes it way up the Bay of Fundy. Unlike most other ghost ships this one will stay in view for up to four hours, something unheard of in ghost ship lore. Other than the extraordinary viewing time, however, the ship conforms to the usual routine of ghost ships. Witnesses report seeing the vision sailing along with flames billowing from each of its masts and debris falling onto the deck and water below. Eventually the masts burn down to the glowing hull and the ship passes gracefully out of view and into legend.

# Dungarvon River

Many years ago there occurred an event on this river that is still talked about to this day. The now famous story of the Dungarvon Whooper is a staple of Maritime lore.

Logging has long had a rich history in New Brunswick and many a ghost story has had its genesis in an isolated logging camp during the long cold nights. The Dungarvon River, which is located in north-central New Brunswick and flows into the Miramichi River, was long an an important highway of logs when this legend was born. But the river wasn't known as the Dungarvon until one morning in the spring of 1850 when logging crews found a serious logjam on the river.

One of the loggers was determined to clear the jam before breakfast and would brook no argument. He was a boastful and foolish fellow by the name of Dungarvon, and he bragged he would clear the jam before breakfast or share it with the Devil in Hell. The cold light of morning was barely on the sky when Dungarvon began his task and before long he was able to free the key logs that were responsible for the large jam. The logs began to move in the current of the river, slowly at first, then at an ever-increasing rate.

The boastful Dungarvon was caught too far from shore and the logs began to move too rapidly for him to jump to safety. He went into the river and under the logs, his broken and lifeless body found downriver sometime later. It wasn't very long afterwards that workers traveling along the logging road that passed the spot of Dungarvon's violent death began to report hearing whooping sounds coming from the river. These eerie sounds could only be heard from a spot directly opposite the site of the logger's death and only early in the morning just as the sun's light begins creeping across the sky. This legend is still told today and some say the unearthly whooping can still be heard early in the morning during logging season on the Dungarvon.

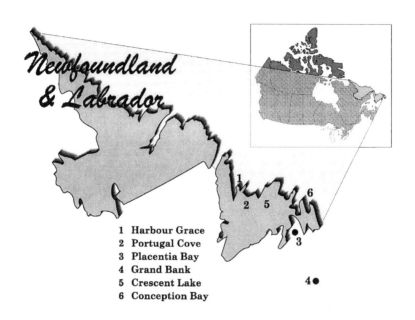

1 Harbour Grace
2 Portugal Cove
3 Placentia Bay
4 Grand Bank
5 Crescent Lake
6 Conception Bay

43

# Newfoundland

## Harbour Grace

Few coastal lands are without legends of derelict ships. Although one of the most famous is that of the *Mary Celeste*, built in Nova Scotia and found abandoned off the Azores in 1872, the legend of the *Resolven* is worth mentioning. The *Resolven* was a brigantine of 145 tonnes that was built in Prince Edward Island. It left Harbour Grace destined for Snug Harbour in late summer 1883, but fate intervened to make sure the *Resolven* would not make land with her crew. She would, however, make the history books.

On August 29, 1883, HMS *Mallard* found the *Resolven* drifting along about eight kilometres east of Catalina on Newfoundland's eastern coast. The *Mallard* hailed her, and when there was no reply, a boarding party was sent over. They found the ship to be deserted. There was a fire still lit in the galley stove, and the captain's logbook was still in his quarters. There was some small damage to the ship, but nothing that put the ship and her crew in peril. So why did the crew abandon the ship? Her lifeboats were gone, but they left the logbook. This meant they may have expected to reoccupy the ship but something unforeseen intervened. A theory was advanced that Captain John James ordered the crew into the lifeboats when an iceberg approached, but whatever the cause, fourteen men disappeared from the *Resolven* one summer day in 1883.

## Portugal Cove

For hundreds of years sailors reported stories of giant sea creatures like the Nordic Kraken, said to crush ships in their tentacles and carry off crews to a horrifying death. Most scientists dismissed these stories as mere folklore, even though one observer in the 1800s was the Prince of Wales. Almost every seaside town has heard the stories, and many a town has found mysterious carcasses washed up on its beaches. In 1877 a giant cuttlefish with tentacles nine metres long washed up on the shore of Trinity Bay, Newfoundland. It was only in the twentieth century that scientists finally recognized the Giant Squid and now hold out the possibility of a Giant Octopus too.

In October 1873, two fishermen were out in Portugal Cove (near Conception Bay) when they saw something unusual floating on the surface of the water. Grabbing a boat hook, one of the men tried to haul it aboard. You can imagine his surprise when he saw it was a giant squid, and a giant squid with an attitude! Two long arms of the creature wrapped themselves around the boat and were in danger of causing it to capsize before one of the fishermen grabbed an axe and cut them off. The giant squid retreated and the remains left on board the ship were measured at six metres. Estimates of the size of the creature ranged from ten to thirteen metres.

## Placentia Bay

Although there has been much speculation in academic circles concerning which ancient peoples reached the New World before Columbus, the Greeks do not usually make the list. The Phoenicians, Romans, Irish, Knight Templars, and Vikings are all rumoured or, in the case of the Vikings, proved, to have reached our shores. So the ghostly wraith that haunts Placentia Bay seems a little out of place.

Fire ships are common along the Atlantic coast, and the flaming vision that disrupts local fishermen shares this factor with its ghastly cousins. For years fishermen have reported seeing a Greek sailing vessel glide across the bay, fully alight, with the screams of its unfortunate victims carrying across the water. Needless to say, this hasn't been conducive to bringing in a large catch, especially since ships close to the apparition can feel the heat of the flames. No one in the area can account for the seemingly out-of-place vision.

## Grand Banks

Tales of giant squids and other mysterious creatures abound on the Grand Banks. Once a place of fantastic riches in all types of fish, the Grand Banks have been over-fished and are just now in the process of recovery. One of the first weird stories out of the Grand Banks occurred in the late 1500s. British explorer Sir Humphrey Gilbert was in command of his ship *Squirrel* plus four others when he observed a creature he described as a "lion to our seeming, in shape, hair, and colour, not swimming after the manner of a beast by moving of his feet, but rather sliding upon the water with his whole body . . . ." The "sea lion" was also described as having long teeth and glaring eyes. It must have been an ill omen, for the *Squirrel* sank a week later.

Another unusual sea animal was sighted on the Grand Banks in 1913. On August 30th the crew of the *Corinthian* spied what they described as a "sea giraffe." From a distance the animal first appeared to be an overturned boat, but as they came within fifty-five metres of it they saw that it was a living animal. The animal then raised its head out of the water about six metres before letting out a wailing noise and disappearing under the waves. The crew of the *Corinthian* were not afraid, though, for they said the creature's eyes were of such a blue colour that it evoked tenderness, not fear, in all who witnessed it.

## Crescent Lake

Though Canadians may already know of the legends of Ogopogo and Champ, there are other lake traditions throughout the country that are just as mysterious. Near the small town of Robert's Arm, Newfoundland, lies Crescent Lake. As with most lake monster traditions, this one begins centuries ago with the Aboriginal tribes in the area. They called this creature *woodun haoot,* which means pond devil. Although periodic reports of Cressie were made throughout the twentieth century, it wasn't until the 1990s that she became a regular feature of the lake.

Now that Cressie has become a familiar sight of the lake a general idea as to her size and shape can be made. She is described as being four to six metres long, black and thin. She does not appear to have any fins or mane. Although the usual explanations are given such as swamp gas and floating logs, local residents are certain that Cressie is a real animal, and they may be right. Large eels have been located in a nearby lake, and there are many stories of divers and swimmers meeting fantastically long eels. Crescent Lake is connected to the Atlantic Ocean by

Tommy's Arm Brook, so it is possible for some of them to migrate to Crescent Lake where they have grown to a large size. They may not be as large as reported, since judging size is especially difficult without the proper cues, but they may be large enough to impress upon local residents that something different inhabits Crescent Lake.

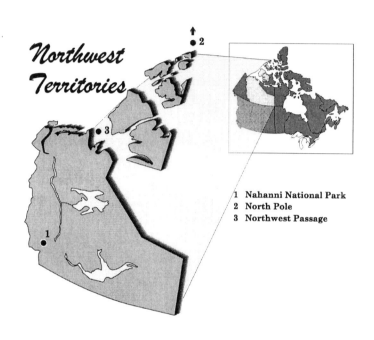

# Northwest Territories

1  Nahanni National Park
2  North Pole
3  Northwest Passage

# Northwest Territories

## The Northwest Passage

The Arctic is a land of stark and rare beauty. It also holds sway as a mystical and mysterious place, so it should come as no surprise that it is home to a rich mythology. The Inuit people of the north have a folklore tradition just as varied and powerful as their southern relatives. Because Inuit folklore is mostly in the form of oral traditions, the major ghost stories of the North come from the European explorers and adventurers who mapped the land and searched for the fabled Northwest Passage, many dying in the attempt. These men have vanished from the stage, but their ships live on in their written logs and memoirs.

The most famous ghost ship of the north could more accurately be called a derelict. And though not in the history books, the *Octavius* was the first ship to find and transit the Northwest Passage. Not that the crew celebrated the feat. They had been dead for years.

The *Octavius* began her fateful journey in September of 1761, when she left England bound for China. She made an uneventful trip around Cape Horn, the southern tip of South America, and up the Pacific to her destination and headed back to England in the fall of 1762. The journey back was not as simple as the one that brought her here. Her skipper decided to take a shortcut and headed for Alaska and the entrance to the Northwest Passage. Since not much was known about the north at this time, he would have been under the impression that the journey would be harsh but not impossible and it would cut months of precious time off the journey. The captain had his wife and ten-year-old son with him, and the sea is no place for families, so perhaps this consideration played some part in his decision. At any rate, the *Octavius* reached Alaska in early November that year.

Thirteen years later the whaling ship *Herald* was becalmed amidst the ice just west of Greenland. It was August but the icebergs were thick as flies at a picnic. The skipper of the *Herald*, Captain Warren, was not concerned until late in the afternoon when a snow squall came up and began to move the ice closer to his ship. It was then that he spied something that would remain with him the rest of his life and would remain a marvel for over the next two hundred years.

The vision that appeared to Captain Warren and his crew made them first think they were seeing a ghost ship. It was a masted ship covered in ice and snow, eerily quiet and coming their way. The captain ordered a boat lowered and eight men as well as the captain made their way to the mysterious ship. As they drew closer they could just make out the faded name *Octavius*. But the name meant nothing to the captain and men who were climbing onto her decks.

They found no life on the upper decks so a search was ordered below. The result of this search would haunt each man the rest of his life. As they made their way into the forecastle they were greeted by the sight of twenty-eight dead men, each one frozen in his bunk, though covered by heavy blankets in a vain attempt to ward off the cold. Leaving this frozen tableau, the men moved aft to the captain's cabin and were met by a further horror. Four more bodies were in the cabin. The captain lay slumped in his chair with his hand on the logbook. His wife lay in her bunk, a frozen stare on her face as she endlessly looked across the cabin at the corpse of a man who had died while trying to light a fire on the floor. Beside him, wrapped in a jacket, was the captain's son.

Captain Warren wanted to remain with the ship to make a proper inspection, but the other eight men were in no mood for that. They convinced the captain to return to the *Herald* with them and as they reached their ship, the *Octavius*, sailed on and out of sight. She would never be seen again.

The *Octavius'* logbook had been brought over to the *Herald*, although part of it had dropped into the sea. It was upon reading the remaining section that Captain Warren made the second startling discovery of the day. He realized that the *Octavius* had reached the opposite part of the continent at Alaska thirteen years before! The logbook said the *Octavius* had been stranded for seventeen days in the ice just north of Port Barrow. They were having trouble keeping a fire lit. Sometime after that final futile attempt the ship had broken free and for the next thirteen years floated through the Arctic waters to a point near Greenland. She had found the Northwest Passage. It would take the living another 130 years to repeat the feat.

Another derelict ship to defy the odds and ice for many years is the *Baychimo*. She comes from another time than the *Octavius* with steel rather than wooden hulls and she made her mark in the history books without her crew.

Launched in 1921 and working for the Hudson's Bay Company out of Vancouver, British Columbia, the *Baychimo* began her strange journey, like the *Octavius*, off Alaska. She was trapped in the ice on October 1, 1931. Captain Cornwall became concerned that the ship might be crushed so he and his crew of sixteen left the ship and made a small camp near shore. Back on board the ship was a million dollars in bundled furs, so the captain made sure the camp was within sight of his ship. She lay trapped in the ice for about a month until a storm that brought warmer weather passed through and snapped her mooring lines, letting her sail away on her own. The crew moved overland to Port Barrow, the captain undoubtedly rehearsing his speech to the company all the way there.

A band of Inuit found her seventy-three kilometres away from the site of her internment and managed to re- move most of her cargo before she sailed away again. She was seen again five months later and almost every year thereafter, including being boarded in 1939. But the *Baychi- mo* always resisted recapture and the final mention of her was in 1956 in the Beaufort Sea where she was seen sail- ing along, completely seaworthy, as if she had important places to go. At that point she had been sailing crewless for twenty-five years. I wonder if she may still be sailing along those cold waters, or if she is held up somewhere waiting for a break in the ice and a chance to resume her endless wandering.

## Nahanni National Park

The next two stories coming to us from the far north have more to do with human desires and fantasies than actual mysteries or ghosts. The first story is reminiscent of Edgar Rice Burroughs' *The Land That Time Forgot*. It is said that there exists a mysterious valley that is a tropical paradise in the cold Arctic. This valley is possible due to hot springs and as a result has the animals one would expect to find in Central America as well as a few that haven't existed for millions of years. Yes, it is a veritable Jurassic Park North. Prehistoric dinosaurs prowl the land and battle daily with the human inhabitants who are ruled by a warrior queen and who protect vast hordes of gold and other precious metals.

If you feel like striking out to find this fabled lost world, the nearest you will come to it will be in Nahanni National Park in the Northwest Territories. The park is a world heritage site and its grandeur and awesome nature befit such a designation. The South Nahanni River flows through the park and the Mackenzie Mountains, resulting in breathtaking rapids. It is amidst this grand spectacle that the mythical lost valley is said to dwell.

In the early 1900s stories began to emerge about a fabled land that was awash in gold nuggets the size of chicken eggs. Needless to say, this prompted some people to strike out in search of these nuggets and the mines that produced them. However, tragedy was the only result, with murder, mayhem and sudden death the more likely outcome to any expedition.

In the 1920s a discovery of large man-made caves spawned the creation of a myth that hairy man-like creatures inhabited the valley and guarded the gold and killed any interlopers. Many more people disappeared trying to find the gold, which seems to have never existed. Many others wrote about the valley and some added elements of mystery and fantastic realms so that the myth of the lost valley today resembles the imaginary land of Edgar Rice Burroughs' tale.

# The North Pole

The second fantastic and fabled land in the north isn't really in the north at all. Rather, the entrance to this fabled land is in the north. Many exotic stories are told of the North Pole and one of the oldest, and oddest, is that the pole is the gateway to the hollow interior of the earth. This Hollow Earth Theory originated in 1692 with Sir Edmund Halley of Halley's Comet fame. In 1720 a publication, *The Christian Philosopher: A Collection of the Best Discoveries in Nature* by Cotton Mather, expanded on this idea and various authors have honed the theory of a hollow sphere ever since. The gateway is said to be three hundred kilometres in diameter.

Basically the Hollow Earth Theory holds that the sphere of the earth is actually hollow, with a sun in the middle, which accounts for the Aurora Borealis. Inside our earth resides a race of humans whom some writers link with the lost tribe of Israel. And of course there are the usual stories of government cover-ups and links with UFOs that serve to prolong this theory well past its Best Before date.

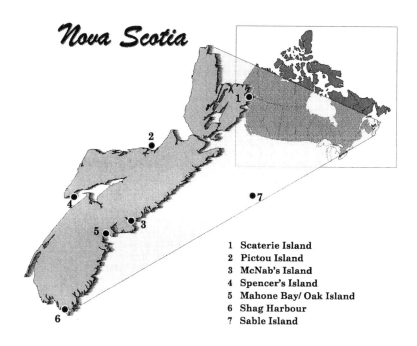

*Nova Scotia*

1  Scaterie Island
2  Pictou Island
3  McNab's Island
4  Spencer's Island
5  Mahone Bay/ Oak Island
6  Shag Harbour
7  Sable Island

# Nova Scotia

Many of the following stories originally appeared in my first book, *Ghosts of Nova Scotia,* although some have been updated or expanded.

## Mahone Bay

One June night in 1813 British warships chased a privateer, *Young Teazer,* into Mahone Bay. The captain torched the magazine and the ship blew up. Since that time, some have seen a blazing ship sailing the bay at night during June and December. The December apparition could be related to the predecessor of the *Young Teazer,* the *Teazer,* which was burned by British ships six months before the *Young Teazer* met her fate. There are also stories of a ball of fire crossing the bay, so it is possible both ships are making an appearance in the still of the night.

# Phantom Ships of Nova Scotia

The Phantom Ship of Northumberland Strait may be the most well known of all Atlantic ghost ships, but it isn't the only one. In Nova Scotia alone, almost every harbour or seaport has its own personal mascot. The following are some of the more well-known ghost ships.

The phantom ship seen near Pleasant Harbour seems concerned with locating a lost treasure from many years ago. It is said that the ship's ghostly complement disembarks from the ship on clear bright nights of the full moon. They drunkenly walk into the woods near Tangier in search of their goal, but mysteriously disappear before they reach it.

The town of Merigomish, Pictou County, may be the setting of two ghost ships. The Phantom Ship of Northumberland Strait makes an appearance here from time to time, but some speak of another ghost ship that suddenly appears and runs aground on an unseen shoal. It bursts into flames and the spectral crew can be seen running through the ship before jumping over the side. The ship then sinks silently into the dark waters.

# Shag Harbour

From Shag Harbour comes one of UFOlogy's greatest mysteries. And as with most mysteries it is part legend, part truth. With the attention being focused on it from around the world, it may yet be possible to determine what happened that cold dark night in 1967.

Shortly after 11 p.m. on October 4, 1967, a large un-identified object with amber-coloured lights was seen descending towards Shag Harbour. Witnesses believed the object was about to plunge into the water, but it was seen to float on the sea just about three hundred metres from the shore, and was apparently drifting with the tide. The object was estimated to be eighteen metres wide and about three metres high with a single, pale yellow light noticeable.

The witnesses notified the local Royal Canadian Mounted Police detachment and they sent two cruisers to the area to investigate. The RCMP and original witnesses believed the craft to be a downed plane and were now concerned with any possible survivors. But before they could notify Search and Rescue in Halifax, or begin to respond with local boats, the object slipped beneath the waves. However, the police and several fishermen did set out for the last seen location of the craft and were surprised to find a half-mile long foamy trail floating on the water about a mile offshore.

The search for survivors from the downed plane came up empty and about an hour later a Canadian Coast Guard cutter came on the scene and reported that all commercial, military and private aircraft were accounted for all the way along the eastern seaboard.

The search then officially ended, but many questions remained. The official RCMP documents and reports referred to the object as a UFO, and the Royal Canadian Air

Force also called it a crashed UFO. In the following year the Condon Report on UFOs would refer to this crash as Case #34 and would classify it as unsolved after looking at all other possible explanations, e.g. meteors, crashed space hardware, etc.

There is a second aspect to this case that has given what is a rather ordinary UFO sighting a twist. It is believed by researchers that the object that crashed into the water at Shag Harbour moved up the coast to Shelburne Harbour where a secret American tracking base was keeping tabs on Soviet submarines. Canadian divers and military personnel scoured the bottom of the harbour and approaches, apparently searching for this object. Some witnesses claim they saw this UFO lying on the bottom conducting repairs. Even a Soviet submarine is rumoured to have started sneaking around until the American and Canadian navies ran it off. Author Don Ledger has explored these stories and has published a book on the subject called *Dark Harbour,* which was published in the spring of 2001. In it he documents the intensive search for the object in Shelburne Harbour that October of 1967, and raises some interesting questions that may yet yield their answers.

# Spencer's Island

Spencer's Island is well known as one of the two best ship-building areas of Nova Scotia. Lunenburg serviced the Atlantic side of the province, while Spencer's Island serviced the Fundy Shore. It is from here that one of the most well-known mysteries of our time began. Ship building was the forte of the people there, but it is one ship in particular that Spencer's Island is famous for.

A brigantine of 287 tonnes, she was built and named the *Amazon* in May 1861. She was thirty-two metres long, but her legend dwarfs many a ship of larger dimensions. Most know her as the *Mary Celeste*. In November 1872, she left New York harbour, bound for Genoa, Italy. At the same time, the British ship *Del Gratia* left New York for Gibraltar. On December 4, the *Del Gratia*, having just come out of a squall, came upon the *Mary Celeste* sailing erratically. Captain Morehouse of the *Del Gratia* became concerned and sent a boarding party to examine the ship. However, the search party found her to be totally deserted, and no reason for her abandonment could be determined. She was in pretty good order, although there were small tears in her sails. Her cargo was still there and many valuables were untouched. A hatch was open, with some water in the hold, but nowhere near enough to have required the crew to abandon ship.

Captain Morehouse sent a crew to the *Mary Celeste* to take her into Gibraltar. Once there, the legal niceties of salvage dragged on for some time as the theories as to what happened developed, and during this century, grew stranger.

Various theories have been put forward to explain the strange disappearance of Captain Briggs, his wife, their daughter, and the crew of the *Mary Celeste*, everything from the Bermuda Triangle, to UFOs, to the *Del Gratia* crew becoming pirates and seizing the ship. This last theory was partially to blame for the long delay in awarding the *Del Gratia* meagre salvage money.

The most likely explanation to the long-standing mystery is that the captain and crew became wary after some of the cargo of alcohol started leaking in the hold. Alcohol fumes are very flammable and it was possible that the crew thought the ship was in mortal danger. They may have taken to the ship's boat and run a line to the ship, but a squall may have developed, and the line may have been broken. A small ship's boat would not last long in the Atlantic and the captain and crew, along with his wife and daughter, would have drowned. The *Mary Celeste* meanwhile would have continued on her way only to be spotted by the *Del Gratia*, and the mystery born. However, exactly what happened that day and the fate of her crew will remain a mystery forever.

As a postscript to this bizarre story, divers who tracked her last voyage and dreamed of finding the mysterious vessel found the wreck of the *Mary Celeste* off Haiti in the summer of 2001. Although the finding of the wreck and possible salvage would in no way settle the questions of the disappearance of her crew, the idea that something of her still remains makes the story alive and real to a new generation of mystery lovers.

# McNab's Island

McNab's Island is one of the last areas of almost un-spoiled beauty in Halifax. It has been used as a place to hang pirates and has had fortifications on it to defend the city, but mostly it is overgrown now, though it does have hiking trails and is accessible only by boat. But it is still occupied by ghosts.

The name McNab's Island comes from Peter McNab who once owned it. He is still there to this day. Upon his death they buried him on the island he loved so much, but legend has it they buried him on one end of the island, with his head buried on the opposite end. Even today his spirit is seen walking the length of the island looking to reclaim his head.

There was once an orphanage on this island and one night it burned down, caused by a candle that got too close to a curtain. Many children were injured or killed and their anguished and frightened cries are said to echo throughout the island. Reports also come down to us of a floating candle seen near the ruins of the orphanage.

There are also reports of a ghostly horse and carriage that is heard making its way across the island on one of the lonely roads.

Finally, this story comes from one of my investigators, Jamie Cox. He has a friend whose family regularly boat over to the island. One time the friend's brother was waiting for the rest to join him in the boat as it was tied up to the dock. He was suddenly startled by sounds of something scraping the length of the underside of the boat. Needless to say he vacated the boat and much later when they brought the boat up onto a dock in Halifax, they saw the keel had been scraped as if by claws . . . .

## Scaterie Island

This large island once housed one of many small settlements that surrounded the French Fortress of Louisbourg on the Atlantic coast of Cape Breton Island. Scatarie Island lies three kilometres off the coast and is surrounded by dangerous shoals and rough waters. It is often shrouded in dense fog, which makes it all the more dangerous to those who pass by. By the look of the island it would be hard to tell that it once had a population of between 200 and 400 people from the 1700s to the 1900s. After the final battle for Louisbourg when the British took complete possession of Nova Scotia in 1758, the French inhabitants of Scatarie Island were forced to leave. The island was renamed Wolfe Island for a time in homage to the British commander who defeated the French at the Plains of Abraham. The new British settlers built houses there, some over old French graveyards. Much of the French presence was obliterated. Or was it?

There have been reports of the ground shaking strangely; of shadows that were taken to be the dead walking the island; of gold buried deep with skeletons on top to scare away looters; of the ghosts of dead mariners appearing two days before their deaths; of gold and more gold, perhaps more gold buried or lost here than anywhere else in Nova Scotia. A fortune may lie beneath the waters around here, and many diving expeditions have been launched searching for that fortune. The legacy of the French inhabitants and their close connection to the Fortress of Louisbourg still remain.

There is also an English ghost story or two to be told.

## Pictou Island

There is apparently a close connection between the Phantom Ship of Northumberland Strait and Pictou Island. This island is located sixteen kilometres north of the town of Pictou on Nova Scotia's northern shore. It is not an especially large island, being only eight kilometres long and three kilometres wide, but it adds a creepy angle to the phantom ship tale.

The ghostly figure of a woman in white is seen walking down a lonely road on the eastern side of the island to a point offshore where a bright, burning light awaits her. When the ghostly woman reaches the light it changes into the now famous sailing ship aglow in flames. As the spectres meet the ship suddenly sinks, and everything is dark and quiet again. This happens mostly at night and after midnight when few are awake and willing to venture too closely to investigate, but sometimes the ghastly woman is seen much closer.

A tale was told of how one day there came a strange knock at the door of one of the homes on the island. The family wasn't expecting anyone and upon opening the door they were greeted by the frightening vision of the resident woman in white. Fear got the best of them and they immediately slammed the door shut without inquiring as to the purpose of this otherworldly visitation. Since then she hasn't attempted any communication with the living. Instead she is content to repeat her walk along that dark lonely road ultimately to meet up with one of the Maritimes' most enduring mysteries.

## Sable Island

Sable Island has a well-earned nickname, Graveyard of the Atlantic. Countless hundreds of vessels have found grief on or around the sandy shore of this island. It is only safe to approach it from one direction in good weather, otherwise the treacherous currents, coupled with dense fogs, the unpredictable weather of the North Atlantic, and dangerous sand bars will doom any attempt. Needless to say, with all this death and destruction legends of a ghostly nature have evolved, even though the island itself is green with small rolling hills.

The first ghost concerns the vision of a fingerless woman. Her name was Mrs. Copeland, and she was a passenger on the ship *Frances* that went down in 1799. There is some dispute as to whether the lady was murdered or not, but it was well known that wreckers (those who made a living off of the unsavoury business of salvaging material and wealth from shipwrecked ships) were sometimes not too concerned with saving the survivors as much as pocketing their valuables. Mrs. Copeland was the wife of Dr. Copeland, Surgeon of the Seventh Regiment based in Halifax. Upon hearing of the loss of the *Frances* (wrongly identified as the *Princess Amelia* in some accounts), a search party was dispatched to the island to determine the fate of the passengers and crew.

It was found that there were no survivors and the wreckage of the *Frances* had been seized and carried away by another ship. After a chase and some detective work, it was discovered that Mrs. Copeland had been buried on Sable Island after her body had washed ashore. The two men who witnessed this and buried her denied killing her, but a legend was created that one of her fingers was cut off to get at a gold ring, and tales have come down about her pitiful ghost roaming the island searching for her missing finger. Fishermen have reported seeing her white wraith gliding among the sand dunes looking for her finger. I wonder why the searchers didn't attempt to retrieve her buried body and answer the questions that have refused to go away to this day?

# Oak Island

The mystery of Oak Island has fascinated dozens of searchers and thousands of armchair adventurers for two hundred years. It is perhaps Nova Scotia's most renowned mystery, and one of the world's most famous. No two people seem to agree on what is buried on Oak Island or who buried it there. The theories range from the mundane to the ridiculous, but at least many have found work and fun investigating this mystery. To understand it we must go back through the cloudy mists of time . . . .

It was the year 1795, and Daniel McInnis visited the island one day as a lark. Oak Island was pretty much only trees then, although some logging had been performed on the island. After walking through the trees, the teenager came upon a clearing. The clearing wasn't new, however, since saplings were growing in place of the trees that were cut down. In the middle of the clearing was an old oak tree with a branch that extended over a small depression in the ground. Accounts differ, but some say that there was an old tackle block that crumbled to the ground when touched hanging from the tree. Daniel realized there was something buried there, and since Nova Scotia's coastline was often the haunt of many a pirate, he made the connection with treasure that has never been broken. The next day he returned with two friends by the name of Vaughan and Smith and they proceeded to dig out the hole. On that day, the Money Pit, as it became known, began to capture the imagination and weave a complicated web.

The boys dug down to a level of three metres before they reached a floor of decaying logs. Excited at this discovery, they pulled up the logs to discover more dirt below. Again they dug and at the six-metre level they again reached a platform of logs. Again they pulled these up and again there was dirt underneath. They finally dug down to the nine-metre level and after pulling that platform of logs up they decided they needed more help. However, it wasn't until 1805 that they were able to convince people to give up their time and effort in a treasure hunt. And when they did all they found were more platforms of logs and a stone tablet that had mysterious markings on it. Some have tried to decipher the markings and one translation read, *Ten feet below, two million pounds are buried.*

Over the years many investors and groups started out with high hopes and good strategies, only to find their hopes dashed by a dose of reality. The table on page 72 lists the various groups, dates and major discoveries over the last two hundred years.

Over the years many theories and theorists have come and gone, and the only constant has been the unshakeable belief in the existence of a treasure. Regardless of what was actually buried on the island, it was of extreme importance to someone for him or her to go through the elaborate precautions of protecting it like this. Almost everything we think of when we think of pirates is actually myth. They rarely held onto their money or booty long enough to bury it, let alone bury it so elaborately. Therefore, it must be something else. However, to be fair I will address the possibility.

| Date | Group | Discoveries |
|---|---|---|
| 1803-04 | Onslow Company | 3 metre x 3 metre chamber at 30 metres |
| 1849-51 | Truro Company | possible chests, pieces of gold chain, built coffer dam to attempt to block sea tunnel |
| 1861-64 | Oak Island Assoc. | proved treasure chamber had dropped into large cavern |
| 1866-67 | Oak Island Eldorado Co. | tried to use coffer dam to block sea tunnel |
| 1878 | Sophie Sellers | |
| 1893-1900 | Oak Island Treasure | cave-in, second water tunnel, reached depth of 51 metres |
| 1909 | Old Gold Salvage & Wrecking Company | drilled to 50 metres |
| 1931 | Chappell | miners seal oil lamp, axe head, pick and anchor fluke |
| 1936-38 | Hedden | stone triangle, collapsed water-tunnel |
| 1938-44 | Edwin H. Hamilton | explored water tunnels |
| 1955 | George J. Greene | pumped 455,000 litres of water into pit which vanished |
| 1959-65 | Robert Restall | found drains at the beach Restall, his son and 2 others died of fumes in the pit |
| 1965-66 | Robert Dunfield | practically dug out the island |
| 1966– | Triton Alliance | a chest and a floating hand were observed via TV around 52 metres |

# The Captain Kidd Theory

Certainly the oldest and most persistent theory of who buried what on Oak Island is that of Captain Kidd. Captain William Kidd was an English privateer who plied the waters of the Atlantic and Caribbean in the 1680s and '90s. In the late 1690s events proved difficult and during an anti-piracy campaign, he strayed over the line into the very act he was out to crush. This, as well as some political maneuvrings and back-stabbing, resulted in his arrest and sentence of death at the gallows.

Just before he met his fate on May 23, 1701, Kidd wrote to the government informing them that he had hidden a great deal of treasure and if they would let him live a little longer, he would lead them to it. This effort was in vain, and the sentence of death was carried out. However, this last plea from the condemned man has resulted in many a treasure hunt around the world and has given Oak Island a ready culprit for the workings on the island.

Alas, however, Captain Kidd did not put anything on Oak Island. There are a couple of reasons for this. First, the crews that Captain Kidd had were a mutinous, criminal bunch with little discipline, certainly not the discipline necessary to build the Money Pit. Second, Captain Kidd's time is almost totally accounted for by historians. There is no gap in the record for the amount of time it took to do what was done on Oak Island, estimated at two years. There is no evidence that Captain Kidd was anywhere near Oak Island at any time.

# The Pirate Theory

The next theory is a related one. Some believe that other pirates buried a remarkable treasure on Oak Island. This theory is given some credence by those that know that pirates frequented Nova Scotia, particularly the La Havre River farther down the coast. However, the classic scene of pirates burying their treasure is not entirely correct. Pirates spent more treasure than they ever buried, and after the few times they did bury some of it, they often came back for it.

That said, there have been small caches of unidentified treasure found from time to time, but nothing as large as the efforts on Oak Island would seem to indicate. Someone spent a lot of time and effort to hide something very large and/or valuable, not just any pickings off any ship. Added to this is the fact that not many pirates had the technical training, time or manpower to do something like Oak Island. Even the idea of a communal bank for pirates doesn't seem logical. Hidden money does no one any good. The whole reason for existence for a pirate was to spend money, not hide it. And it's doubtful that many pirates would trust one another enough to develop a communal bank for their treasure. As a final nail in the pirate communal bank coffin, no whisper or hint of such a thing has ever surfaced, and not all pirates died early deaths. Someone would know and come looking.

# The Francis Bacon Theory

The next theory is really a hard sell. You first have to believe that William Shakespeare didn't really write all those plays attributed to him. The theory is that Sir Francis Bacon did and that he felt he must hide his authorship of the plays for political reasons. Because of his Masonic connections with the major explorers and developers of the New World, he decided to hide the manuscripts on a deserted island far away from palace intrigue.

There is no evidence that Francis Bacon wrote any of the Shakespearean material. Some scholars seem to find it impossible to believe that someone with limited education and no great political connections could write the beautiful works that we believe William Shakespeare wrote. These scholars seem to forget that there are many instances of people coming out of nowhere to do great things. What is this bias against a common person achieving greatness? It is almost like they wish to steal more glory for a man who has more than his share already. And as one writer commented, if you read any of Bacon's work, then you'll know for sure he didn't write Shakespeare's.

Now, even if I could subscribe to the theory that Francis Bacon really did the writing, I must believe that he buried his manuscripts underground guarded by water tunnels. Paper . . . water, hmm. Doesn't seem logical to me, although some people bring up the idea out that the manuscripts were secured in liquid mercury to preserve them. Still, the only evidence for the fact that there is something of a paper product down there is the tiny fragment of parchment brought up with one of the drills. I can think of a simpler reason why there would be a parchment down there. Obviously there would be a manifest listing the total of whatever is buried and perhaps its worth. This is a far less complicated reason for finding paper down there.

As for the Masonic connections, practically everyone in power in England back then, and the men they sent out to discover and develop the new lands, was a Mason. I don't think you could find an explorer during that time who wasn't a Mason or connected with one. It would be like meeting someone in Rome and finding it funny that he or she was a Catholic. A rule to live by in areas of the paranormal or mysterious is that you never try to explain one unknown with another, such as Bigfoot coming from UFOs.

## The Bloodline of Jesus Christ Theory

The next theory is almost as complicated as the Bacon one, but at least it has circumstantial evidence backing it up. Essentially, it states that the treasure is from the Knights Templar, a religious sect that fought in the Crusades and became so rich that many of the monarchs of Europe went to them in time of need. In the fourteenth century, the king of France went to the pope and convinced him to outlaw the Templars and thus in a sneak attack, the king's men stormed their castles and arrested, tortured and killed many of them. At the Templars strongest stronghold, they were able to hold out long enough to spirit some of their massive treasure away, and it has never been found.

Many Templars made for Scotland and were welcomed there. In 1395, the Earl of Orkney likely made a transatlantic journey to Nova Scotia, and some scholars have tried for a connection between the Earl and the Templar treasure. However, nothing is certain, although much of it is plausible and could have happened that way.

A variation on the theme of the Templars has them hiding either the Holy Grail, the chalice of the Last Supper, or the Holy Grail, the bloodline (descendants) of Jesus Christ. There is also the theory that the Holy Grail is actually the original receptacle of the Shroud of Turin. Again, there is much circumstantial evidence to link the Templars to the descendents of Jesus Christ and secret societies, and Samuel de Champlain. Coincidentally, Champlain was meticulous in his charting the region of the Maritimes, yet he became vague in the area around Oak Island. Interesting . . . .

## The Pay-Ship Theory

This next theory is that a pay-ship of the British, French or Spanish navies was caught in a storm and washed ashore near Oak Island. The commanders decided to bury the treasure until they could return with a stronger force. Although pay ships of the various navies did founder along the Atlantic coast of North America, and one French ship did make for Halifax's Bedford Basin, there is no evidence to directly link any missing money and the diggings on Oak Island. However, this theory has the strength of at least picking the right people who did the job.

## The French/English Theory

A variation on the pay-ship theory is that the French felt their holdings in Acadia were in jeopardy, as they were, and hid some of their money until things cleared up. Of course when they did, the French were out.

Another variation is that the English did much the same, or hid some of the money they would need to fight the colonists. But in this case, why didn't they ever come back for it? Nova Scotia was always under their control and they could have come and retrieved the treasure at any time.

## The Sack of Havana Theory

This next theory again is very similar to the hide-the-stuff-until-it's-safe theories, except that they wanted it safe from the tax man, so to speak.

This theory holds that after the Sack of Havana in 1752, the leaders of the successful British invasion-cum-looting of Havana decided to skim off some of the take before sending it back to King George III. A variation along these lines is that George didn't trust his ministers, since he was relatively new to the job, and wanted some money hidden away for a rainy day, so to speak. Then he lost his mind, and the money as well. But what of the men who organized and buried the treasure?

## The Sir William Phips Theory

This theory is the newest, just being published in *Oak Island and its Lost Treasure* in 2000. Authors Graham Harris and Les MacPhie summarize the story thus far, then propose that Sir William Phips, sea captain and adventurer, procured a treasure from a wreck off the Bahamas and hid it from James II.

King James was not the most popular monarch ever to sit on the English throne, and some thought it was only a matter of time before William of Orange would invade from the continent and assume the throne. Phips had been sent out by Charles II (brother of James II) in 1683 to locate the wreck of the Spanish ship *Concepcion* in the Bahamas, which was rumoured to have been loaded with four to six million pesos. This was a time when the continental powers were rivals to drain the New World of her riches as fast as humanly possible. Consequently, the Caribbean is strewn with the wrecks of many well-loaded ships just waiting to be recovered. The idea appealed to Charles and so the royal command was given.

Sir William Phips was a sea captain out of Boston who had married well and was able to rise above his impoverished beginnings. He was an ambitious man who was twice responsible for attacks upon New France and thus knew the waters of Acadia well. He set out in 1683 on the *Rose of Algeree* but his first expedition amounted to little more than a reconnaissance in force. It wasn't until his second expedition in 1686 that he located the wreck and began salvage operations. Charles had died in the meantime and his brother James had succeeded to the kingship. James was Catholic and was in secret negotiations with the king of France to make England Catholic again. Thus the trouble with the Protestant William of Orange.

## The Most Likely Suspects

I have not included every theory as to who buried what on Oak Island. I purposely left out the fantastic, impossible or ridiculous, and concentrated on the theories that at least had a chance of being right, even if the Bacon one is a real stretch. No, the person who dreamed up this adventure, planned and engineered it and executed the world's greatest secular mystery was military or pseudo-military. Because of this, I would probably reject the Templars as well as Bacon. This was a military job by either the French or, more likely, the British. It took two years and massive manpower to construct a trap for the curious. Obviously, it was never meant for anyone to go back down the same way it was put there. There is some trick to it and it is possible, even likely, that the treasure ended up a short distance away just under the ground ready for easy access.

The Money Pit is meant as a trap to take the curious off the scent. Even the likely treasure chests found through the drilling were probably a sacrificial lamb in case anyone succeeded in getting down that far. Can you imagine going through all this trouble for two treasure chests? No, whatever was or is on Oak Island must have been massive, either in wealth or importance.

The only way to find out who put the treasure there on the island is to search history for the likely suspects, the men who had the capability and disappeared for about two years. Find them, and you find the likely reason for their efforts. Understand the reason for their efforts, and you have the treasure, at least in your mind. It is possible that the treasure could only be found by unravelling the clues scattered throughout the island, and at some time in the past, someone did. Does it not strike anyone as strange that something of this magnitude could stay a secret for so long? Someone must have told someone. Husbands tell wives or families. Families leave letters or papers behind after deaths. There has never been a mention or whisper of the treasure. We have no idea of what it is. Therefore, either the men who buried it did not know what it was they were burying, or else they came back and got it. The *Titanic* became famous for sinking. Her sister ship, the *Olympic*, made five hundred crossings of the Atlantic and no one knows her name. If the treasure was still there, it would be like an unfinished journey of the greatest magnitude, and there would be some trail. If not, if they came back for it, then it was just another secret military project.

Ho-hum. Dime a dozen, just another rambling of Grandpa about his youthful experiences in the navy. Wouldn't that be a kick in the teeth!

Also seen on Oak Island are the ghostly apparitions of sixteenth- and seventeenth-century soldiers. They walk the roads, woods and beaches, still guarding or searching for something. Pirates' apparitions are also seen or heard from time to time on the island. Are they the ones who buried something here, still looking for their treasure?

## Nova Scotia's Haunted Lakes

In Nova Scotia it seems almost every lake is inhabited or haunted by some spirit or creature (see *Ghosts of Nova Scotia*). Although much of this can be attributed to local folktales and mystical beliefs, it seems there may actually be something going on under the waves.

Cape Breton Island has some of the more beautiful lakes I have ever seen. The Bras d'Or Lakes take up almost all the centre of the island and, besides being noted for boating and golf, in a province where almost every lake is said to have some creature or spirit associated with it, the area is also home to some of the more interesting ghost stories I have ever heard.

Lake Ainslie, which is in the western part of Cape Breton, is also known for its mysteries and ghosts. In particular, the lake monster said to inhabit its cool waters is described as being whale-like with a couple of humps. Estimates vary, but reports of three to six metres are common. It is also described as being dark coloured and shy. Some scientists think they may be able to account for this rare beast. First proposed in 1966 by Dr. Carl Medcof, the theory is that the Lake Ainslie monster is actually a case of eel-balls being sighted in the lake. Eels do come together and form a sizable mass that, if surfacing, can appear large and hump-backed. However, this theory fails to satisfy those who have seen the "monster" of Lake Ainslie.

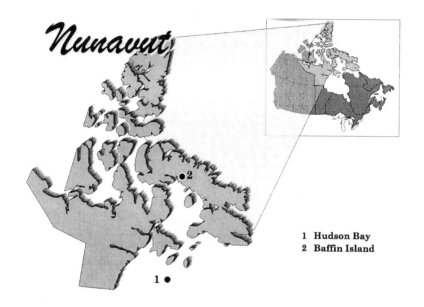

*Nunavut*

1 Hudson Bay
2 Baffin Island

# Nunavut

## Hudson Bay

Hudson Bay is a massive inland sea that was named for explorer Henry Hudson who entered it in his ship the *Discovery* in 1611. As with most explorers of the north, Hudson was looking for the Northwest Passage, but found only hardship and death instead. It was on June 23, 1611, that his crew mutinied and cast Hudson, his son, and seven followers adrift, while they made for home. There is some speculation that Hudson may have survived for some time among the Native tribes.

Those people who may have sheltered Hudson tell us of other less welcome visitors that haunt the shores of Hudson Bay, Quebec, and Labrador. The Adlet are a humanoid race of wolf-like creatures that stand about two-and-a-half metres tall and weigh anywhere from ninety to 140 kilograms. Although they are of the approximate height of the Sasquatch and are covered in fur, these creatures bear closer resemblance to a werewolf with their wolfish faces, long fangs, and endless hunger for blood.

The Adlet were spawned by an abominable marriage of an Inuit woman and a red dog. The woman had ten children of this hideous union. Half of them looked like normal canines, the other five were a horrible hybrid of canine and human. These were the Adlet, and they had nasty dispositions. They attempted to kill their mother and only the intervention of their father saved her and the other five children. The red-dog father was killed while the mother and the other five children escaped, leaving the Adlets to the elements.

The Adlets survived their ordeal and are said to still stalk the Arctic shores looking for prey. Omnivorous, the Adlet can subsist on any food they can find in the north, but prefer to hunt humans for their warm blood and tasty innards. As with traditional stories of werewolves, silver bullets are said to be effective in killing these abominations.

# Baffin Island

From Baffin Island come tales of two humanoid races that existed thousands of years ago. One was a race of fierce giants called the Tunis and the other was a race of fierce pigmies called the Skraeling.

The Skraeling play a prominent role in Norse mythology and are blamed for making the Norse relinquish their hold on North America along the Atlantic Coast around Newfoundland and the Maritimes. Skraeling means "screamer" and refers to the nasty habit these beings had as they attacked the Norse settlements around 1000 AD.

The Tunit were said to be terrifying giants who attempted to enslave the Inuit until they were defeated and driven out of the north. Whether any of this is true or if it is related to the stories of giant man-like primates of the west coast and Alberta is little more than speculation at this time. However, if we do allow ourselves to speculate for a moment, it is possible that if Sasquatch reached North America via the Bering Strait, like the ancestors of the Inuit and Native tribes to the south, then they could have reached the Northwest Territories also. However, it should be noted that the present day behaviour of Sasquatch does not match the fierce reputation of the Tunit.

# Arctic rivers

Prowling the banks of many Arctic rivers is said to be a horrible creature. More properly identified as a ghoul, this animated corpse goes in search of hapless victims and drowns them. The Ahkiyyinni is a rotting cadaver determined to wreak vengeance upon his tormentors.

The Ahkiyyinni began life as any other Inuit hunter. It wasn't until after his death that the Ahkiyyinni crossed over into the realm of the terrible. While alive, the Ahkiyyinni loved to dance and was well known throughout the North. But being good at anything is sure to cause jealousy in others, and so it was in this case.

One day a group of young hunters sailed past the Ahkiyyinni's grave and mocked him and his love for dancing. They made a cruel joke of how difficult it must be for the young hunter to dance while entombed in the cold earth. This was too much for the Ahkiyyinni and he crawled out of his grave to laugh at the frightened hunters in their boat. He was a horrible sight to see with his rotting flesh, sunken black eyes and protruding ribs. As he walked along the shore his footsteps rumbled underneath him. Then he began to dance as the young hunters pleaded for their lives and his cruel smile presaged their deaths. The thundering of his footsteps caused the waters to boil and the boat was capsized, drowning the foolish hunters who dared malign the dead.

It is said he roams the northern rivers, never straying too far or he will be entombed again. He is consumed with jealousy, directed at the living who can still enjoy life while he is a rotting abomination. Upon seeing the living, Ahkiyyinni begins his dance of death, which sends a cascade of cold, dark water over his victims, robbing them of the life he yearns for so deeply.

1   Lake Simcoe
2   Georgian Bay
3   Manitoulin Island
4   Niagra Falls
5   Memeigwess Lake
6   Toronto Harbour
7   Cove Island Light
8   Thunder Bay

# Ontario

## Lake Simcoe

Each summer visitors travel to Barrie or Orillia in order to catch a glimpse of the monsters that are said to inhabit Lake Simcoe. There is some discussion as to whether there are actually two separate monsters, commonly known as Igopogo and Kempenfelt Kelly, or if the sightings are of two different genders. Lake Simcoe has some of the highest reported numbers of sightings of lake monsters in North America. However, many sightings are diametrically opposite from each other, so there is obviously more than one factor involved in the generation of reports from this area.

Igopogo is described as being nine to twenty-one metres long with dorsal fins, a dog-like face, and dark gray or black colouring. Kempenfelt Kelly is variously described as being plesiosaur-like, worm-like, or dolphin-like. Reports agree it has flippers, large eyes, long length, and dark colouring. However the creature(s) really look, they are certainly a big draw for tourists, and a boon for the local economy.

# Georgian Bay

## Yeo Island

An unusual ghost is said to haunt this island in Georgian Bay. In 1828 the British schooner *Hackett* was dispatched to Drummond Island in order to facilitate the movement of troops and supplies from the fort on the island to a new home. As well as human cargo, pigs, sheep, and horses were stowed aboard the schooner. During the journey to their new home a ferocious storm blew up and the ship was run aground on Fitzwilliam Island. The crew and most of the passengers abandoned the ship, but a woman, her child and the animals were left aboard. The next day the survivors returned and rescued the poor ones left through the freezing night on the schooner.

All the survivors, as well as a horse named Louie, made it to Yeo Island where they awaited rescue. It came within a few days, but there was no room for Louie the horse. Poor Louie was left on the lonely, desolate island to fend for himself. For a time afterward the island was called Horse Island in honour of its singular resident. Finally, after Louie was no more, the island's name returned to Yeo, but Louie was not forgotten. Sailors passing the island reported the vision of a white horse could be seen racing along the shore. Louie spends his eternity as he spent the last months of his life, alone.

## Cove Island Light

Cove Island is situated at the entrance to Georgian Bay from Lake Huron. The lighthouse in question was established in 1858 to cover some of the most treacherous shoals and rocks found in the Great Lakes. It is believed that the light is haunted by one Captain Amos Tripp.

Captain Tripp was in command of the schooner *Regina* one storm-lashed day in October of 1881. The ship began to take on water, and although Captain Tripp attempted to beach her on a sandbar, the schooner sank, taking Tripp with her. The captain's body was recovered and unceremoniously buried along the shore, and some believe this has caused his spirit to return to the lighthouse. Legend has it Captain Tripp returns when there is a strong north wind and plays cards with the light-keeper. Another legend has it that Tripp returned one stormy night when the light had gone out and relit it in time to save a ship from certain destruction. In either case, it seems certain that Captain Tripp wishes to intervene and save others from his ghastly fate.

## Giants Tomb Island

This island, which is a part of the Georgian Bay Islands National Park, has a legend that is a creepy as its name. It is said that the island is the final resting place of a giant known in native lore as Kı-chı-kı-wa-na. Known to Europeans as Rockman, this terrific creature was the last of a race of giants, some of whom were known to throw icebergs around like snowballs. The many islands in Georgian Bay are said to have come about when Rockman slipped and fell into the bay, shattering the rock into many pieces. Even with that accident Rockman's love of the area wasn't dimmed and he spent the remaining time of his life on the island. The local natives buried him with respect and left offerings to his spirit, but only during the day. They would not approach the island at night in case they disturbed his sleep. An admonition that holds to this day.

## Niagara Falls

Niagara Falls is the honeymoon destination for thousands of people each year. The falls, first seen in 1678 by the Belgian missionary Louis Hennepin, are magnificent, and the history behind their creation is quite fascinating. They have moved eleven kilometres in the past 10,000 years to their present location. The Niagara River is the largest river in the world by volume of water passing through it, and to walk the banks of this river below the falls is an amateur geologist's heaven. The river itself forms the international boundary between the United States and Canada. The falls and the river are also quite fascinating for another reason. Niagara Falls is one of the most haunted places in Canada. Most of its ghosts are landborne but a few water related stories are of concern to us.

Niagara Falls is known for other things than just a nice place to spend your honeymoon. It is also known as a place that has a strange force that connects it with death, particularly suicide. Perhaps it is the easy access to the falls, or maybe the glitter and happiness that surrounds the falls is too much to take for the lonely and downtrodden. Regardless, many have chosen the falls as their final point of departure from this life. Some have been unwillingly drawn by the sight and sound of the water and have almost succumbed to its hypnotic call. Perhaps it is this call that has given rise to a legend that the Seneca and Neutral Natives who once lived in the area once practiced human sacrifice at the falls. Either way, Niagara Falls certainly has a siren call for many, both in a positive and negative way.

A Canadian National Railroad overpass tunnel has been immortalized in both a Hollywood film and a ghost legend. *The Dead Zone* was released in 1983 and one scene took place at the CNR tunnel in northern Niagara Falls. Just off Warner Road is the tunnel that some say is haunted by the ghost of a girl who burned to death fleeing from a burning barn. Her cries are said to echo from the tunnel when you light a match and it was this legend that drew the Hollywood film crew here for the scene from *The Dead Zone*.

From the American side of the falls comes a story of a curse that affects those who visit an eerie cave located between the Whirlpool and Lewsiton, New York. This cave is a natural limestone formation about eight metres deep and is as dark and dreary as most caves. It is a part of the Devil's Hole State Park and is a quite popular destination for tourists. But most don't know its dark history.

The Seneca believed the cave was the home to an evil spirit and warned 17th-sentury explorer René-Robert Cavelier de La Salle not to explore it. Being the intrepid voyageur, and not one to listen to superstitious stories from "ignorant Indians," LaSalle entered the cave and was plagued with misfortune for the rest of his life.

Those same Senecas massacred settlers and soldiers here in 1763. President William McKinley passed close to the cave in 1901 and was assassinated that same day. A train car with fifty souls aboard left the tracks and plunged into the Niagara River, killing most of the passengers. And countless people over the past few hundred years have fallen in the cave and died. Perhaps it is no wonder that many only speak of the cave in whispers.

Perhaps the most well known spectre, at least by name, is that of the Maid of the Mist. Her name is carried on one of the tour boats that takes tourists to the falls, but she is also the legend of a Native girl who preferred death to a hated marriage. She rode her canoe over the falls but was saved at the last moment by the Native God *He-No*, the Thunderer. He carried her to his cave, which is hidden by the mist of the falls, but from time to time you can see her reflection in the water as she peers out through the deluge. There is another version of this story, which is quite similar, but the girl's name is Lewlaw-la, and her father or brokenhearted lover, follows her over the falls. Her image is also said to be visible through the mists at the foot of the falls.

# St. Lawrence River's Watery Ghost Towns

Prior to the opening of the St. Lawrence Seaway system in 1959, many small towns were abandoned due to the on-coming flood as the changes in the St. Lawrence River were made. These towns were submerged and have been forgotten by the world at large. Only the former residents and some of those who live along the new banks of the St. Lawrence care to think about the once thriving communities far below in their watery graves.

Divers have been the only visitors to these ghost towns and some have reported strange feelings and sights when they have been down there. Some people believe the former residents of these watery towns have come back and can be seen going about their daily work as if time had no meaning, which it doesn't to a ghost. Many sailors who have passed over these relics have reported strange lights far below and voices that come to them from below the waves. The towns of Moulinette, Dickinson's Landing,

Aultsville, Milles Roches, Farran's Point, and parts of Iroquois and Morrisburg may still exist for apparitions of their former residents.

## Memeigwess Lake

This lake east of Dryden is home to two waterborne legends. The first concerns a sighting of the Wendigo. Described as a devil, he is said to inhabit a cave at the eastern end of the lake in the side of a cliff. This ancient tale still frightens the locals and not many will venture to the den of this powerful demon to challenge the legend.

Also seen nearby are the Maymaygwayshi. These petite creatures seem related to the Nagumwasak of the Atlantic Coast and, indeed, some researchers believe the legend may originate with stories of the Vikings from the coast. However, I don't think small or petite was ever an adjective applied to the Vikings. In fact, the Maymaygwayshi are described as extremely ugly, hairy, and monkey-like. They are said to be ashamed of their looks and hide in caves or rock faces along the shores of Memeigwess Lake and nearby Indian Lake. The only time they are seen is when they are caught out fishing, but some natives still leave offerings for good luck by their suspected lairs.

# The Great Lakes

## Lake Ontario

Lake Ontario is the smallest and most easterly of the Great Lakes. It is 311 kilometres long and at its widest it reaches 133 kilometres. Lake Ontario lies almost perfectly along the east/west axis and has a surface area of 19,554 square kilometres. If the whole drainage basin is taken into account, the area rises to 70,400 square kilometres. The Niagara River is the main feeder river. Although the lake reaches a depth of 244 metres, its average depth is 86 metres. Lake Ontario is connected to Lake Erie by the Welland Canal and the Niagara River.

### Toronto Harbour

One of the first lighthouses established around Lake Ontario has sat at Gibraltar Point since 1808. It is of sturdy construction and stands twenty-five metres high. Being one of the oldest landmarks in Toronto, it has its share of legend and history. One of these legends has continued into the present day.

The first lighthouse keeper was a man by the name of J.P. Raden Muller, who cared for the structure from 1809 till 1815. Raden Muller was known for his fine brewing skills, and people from all around knew the good quali-

| Ghost Ships of the Great Lakes | |
|---|---|
| **Lake Ontario** | Bavaria<br>Hamilton<br>French Yawl |
| **Lake Huron** | Celtic<br>Water Witch<br>Keystone State<br>Eclipse<br>Kate L. Bruce |
| **Lake Michigan** | Alpena<br>Chicora<br>Ella Ellenwood<br>Ellen Spry*<br>Jamestown<br>Orphan Boy*<br>William Sanderson* |
| **Lake Erie** | Gray Ghost<br>Lady Elgin<br>Griffin<br>Jane Miller (Georgian Bay)<br>South America |
| **Lake Superior** | Hudson<br>Bannockburn<br>Edmund Fitzgerald<br>Selvick<br>City of Detroit<br>Jane Miller<br>Emperor<br>Lambton |

* Mary Celesete type vessel

ty of his beer. Also situated on Gibraltar Point was a blockhouse manned by soldiers from Fort York. One night the drunken soldiers demanded Rademuller share his brew with them, but he attempted to reason with them instead, trying to get them to sleep it off. This enraged the men, and one of the soldiers beat Raden Muller with a club, and the others joined in to throw the poor man to his death from the top of the lighthouse. They then chopped him up and buried him along the point.

The authorities couldn't have been too bright because they never found out Raden Muller was the victim of foul play until 1832 when a lightkeeper by the name of James Durnam discovered his bones buried close to the lighthouse. Durnam claimed he could see and hear the ghost of poor Raden Muller on foggy nights, howling in agony and searching for his murderers.

Today the belief in the ghostly goings-on continues. Raden Muller's footsteps and moans are said to still echo through the structure, while strange shadows and cloudy manifestations are regularly seen. One night a reporter for a local newspaper decided to stay at the lighthouse. Being of a skeptical nature, he searched the premises before settling down to his vigil. On an inspection of the lighthouse he noticed plaster had fallen onto the steps, lightly covering them in a white powder. He cleaned the steps, but on his next inspection, the powder was back. Not only that, but there was a faint set of footprints on the stairs even though he was alone that night. No mention is made of geologic disturbances that could have loosened the plaster, and no mention is made of whether the reporter left the lighthouse as skeptical as he entered.

## Toronto Harbour Revisited

There is a delightful story in Frederick Stonehouse's *Haunted Lakes: Great Lakes Ghost Stories, Superstitions and Sea Serpents* of a ghost ship that was seen in 1913.

Apparently in the summer of that year Rowley W. Murphy, a historian and artist, was sailing his small boat into Toronto Harbour. Ahead of him he noticed another small boat of a similar size, but noticeably out of date. As he got within fifteen metres of this old boat he saw that its three occupants were the worse for wear. Their clothes were not only of an older time, but they looked as if they were in the process of being worn right off the body. The boat was seen to be taking on water, yet it remained afloat with the occupants unconcerned, just staring off into the distance, as if looking for a shore they would never see. Because one of the men was wearing an old tri-coloured hat, Murphy guessed it was a French vessel from many years ago. Soon it drifted off into the night and he never saw it again.

## McCoy Islands

An eerie experience awaits those who approach this island during a full moon in September. Located north of Parry Sound, the McCoy Islands are surrounded by dangerous shoals and reefs that could spell doom for the unwary. But the wary never approach these islands in September when the moon is full. There once was an old trader named McCoy who would cheat or steal from anyone, either friend or stranger. And McCoy was ahead of his time in that he wasn't prejudiced, because he stole from white man or Native with equal ease. It doesn't come down to us which race finally had enough with the dishonest trader, but someone took their revenge late one September night and since then those who sail by the islands speak of the terrible screams that can be heard echoing around the islands.

## Lake Erie

Lake Erie is the fourth largest of the Great Lakes at 56,725 square kilometres for the entire drainage basin. Its mean depth is the smallest at fifty-eight metres and its deepest point is 244 metres. The lake is connected to Lake Huron by the Detroit River and to Lake Ontario by the Niagara River and Wellend Canal. The Canadian province of Ontario is to the north of the lake and the American states of Michigan, Ohio, Pennsylvania, and New York lie to the south.

The first European to see the lake is usually credited as French-Canadian explorer Louis Jolliet in 1669, although there are some researchers who believe that French explorer Étienne Brûlé reached here in 1615. The Iroquois were the primary Native tribe to inhabit the region prior to this (although the lake is named after the Erie Natives who once lived here also), and the English became the primary developers and explorers afterwards. There was a major naval battle on Lake Erie during the futile War of 1812 (actually 1812-1814). The American Commodore Oliver H. Perry defeated the British in an engagement at Put-in-Bay, Ohio.

## The Griffin

French explorer René-Robert Cavilier Sieur de La Salle, who was instrumental in opening up commercial trade in the Great Lakes, was also instrumental in building a ship that would earn the earliest title of the "Flying Dutchman" of the Great Lakes. The *Griffin* was launched in 1679 with the full intention of making the run between Lakes Erie and Michigan. She reached Green Bay, Michigan, and departed for Niagara on September 18, but fate intervened and she sailed into mystery instead. No sign was ever found of her. This isn't all that surprising since much of the Great Lakes were untouched by humans.

Many people have claimed to have found the wreck, but her final resting place is still a mystery. A lighthouse keeper on Manitoulin Island in Lake Huron found five human remains in a cave, one of which was a large skeleton. The pilot of the *Griffin* was an especially large Danish man, so some suspected the remains could be that of some of the *Griffin*'s survivors. With a remarkable lack of respect the keeper gave most of the bones away to tourists and friends. Perhaps that is why some claim to see the

*Griffin* sailing along from time to time in Lake Michigan and Lake Erie. Not only may some of her crew be looking to finally make port, but some may be looking for their bones.

## Lake Huron

Lake Huron is the second largest of the Great Lakes with a drainage basin of 129,250 square kilometres and a length of 332 kilometres. It has a maximum width of 252 kilometres. It has a maximum depth of sixty-four metres and is connected to Lake Superior by the St. Mary's River and Lake Michigan via the Straits of Mackinac. Georgian Bay, at its eastern end is three hundred kilometres long and 125 kilometres wide, with a range of depth from 250 to 1,350 metres. There are many rivers draining into Georgian Bay, including the Severn from Lake Simcoe.

Georgian Bay Islands National Park contains more than forty islands in the western and southwestern part of the bay.

Although the middle lake and the third most westerly, Lake Huron was the first of the Great Lakes to be seen by Europeans. Samuel de Champlain and Étienne Brûlé reached Georgian Bay in 1615. Louis Jolliet passed through Lake Huron in 1669 on his way to Lake Erie. The lake was named after the native Huron tribes around the lake.

## Manitoulin Island

A particularly gruesome story comes to us from this island in northern Lake Huron. Apparently many years ago two soldiers of the British Empire were stationed on Drummond Island and found life in the desolate winter too much to bear. They unwisely decided to desert their posts and their commander put a bounty on their heads. Now this was not legal, even in those days, but a couple of natives decided to take on the task and make themselves a tidy sum of twenty dollars. They tracked down the two unwary deserters and located them on Great Manitoulin Island where they laid in wait until the right moment. Surprise was total and the two men were dozing by a fire when the natives relieved them of their heads and took them back to their commander for the bounty.

Legend has it that the two headless bodies can still be seen warming themselves by a fire, or wandering the shore looking for their heads. Many a fisherman or unwary traveler has been horrified to come upon this gruesome and bloody sight.

## Lake Superior

Lake Superior is the largest and most westerly of the Great Lakes. It has a drainage area of 123,250 square kilometres with a length of 563 kilometres. At its greatest width it reaches four hundred kilometres, and has a maximum depth of 406 metres. Superior is bounded by Ontario in the east and north and the American states of Michigan, Minnesota and Wisconsin in the west and south. There are about two hundred rivers that drain into the lake. Lake Superior is often called the prettiest of the Great Lakes, particularly in the north which has many deep bays and high cliffs. Étienne Brûlé was the first European to visit the lake in 1622, and Claude-Jean Allouez, a Jesuit missionary and explorer, first charted the lake in 1667. The British gradually gained control over the lake between 1763 and 1783. The name comes from the French Lac Suprieur, which means Upper Lake.

## Thunder Bay

Many a sailor believes in a "hoodoo ship." Some ships just seem to be unlucky. Other sailors believe in "hoodoo areas" much like the non-existent Bermuda Triangle.

Rarely does it seem the two beliefs combine, but between 1905 and 1913 three out of four sister ships from the Algoma Central Railroad were wrecked near Thunder Bay.

The *Monkshaven* was the first to go, being wrecked on Pie Island in November of 1905. The next was the *Theano*, which pulled a similar trick on Trowbridge Island in November of 1906. The third, the *Leafield*, disappeared in November, 1913. Three sister ships were wrecked or disappeared in the same general area in the same month, albeit different years. More than enough evidence for some that there are jinxed ships and seas.

# The Bannockburn

Probably the best known "Flying Dutchman" ghost ship is that of the *Bannockburn*, a 1,650-tonne, 75-metre steamer built in 1893 and designed to fit through the Welland Canal. In November of 1902 the *Bannockburn* was en route to Sault Ste. Marie when she disappeared shortly after passing another ship. Despite a detailed search along her projected path, nothing was ever found of the steamer. Various theories were advanced, but without any evidence, such as a wreck, none of them were more than educated guesswork. Eventually an oar and lifejacket were found, but neither was conclusively determined to be from the *Bannockburn*.

It was little more than a year after she disappeared when whispered stories began that she could still be seen sailing Lake Superior, trying to make port. The *Bannockburn* was first seen sailing past Caribou Island on her way to Sault Ste. Marie, much as she would normally have appeared had she been real. Later, people would swear they saw her encrusted in a soft, glowing sheet of ice and this became the usual description of her cited by many a sailor on a cold dark night, especially in the stormy month of November.

# The Edmund Fitzgerald

*The legend lives on from the Chippewa on down*
*Of the great lake they called Gegchugume*
*The lake it is said never gives up her dead*
*When the skies of November turn gloomy*

> – Gordon Lightfoot, "The Wreck of the Edmund Fitzgerald"

Perhaps the most famous wreck of the past twenty-five years is that of the *Edmund Fitzgerald*, immortalized by Gordon Lightfoot in his haunting ballad from 1976.

The ship went down in November of 1975, another victim of the "witch of November," and might have remained just another unfortunate casualty of Lake Superior's fury if not for some intriguing "coincidences." Taken together, they have started a legend that the ship still plies the waters of this turbulent lake, still trying to make it to Sault Ste. Marie.

Soon after her sinking the *Edmund Fitzgerald's* final resting place became a natural beacon to the curious. Jacques Cousteau led a mission to the site in 1980 and rumour has it the crew were scared off by mysterious lights seen shining from the pilothouse. Lights can play weird tricks on the human mind, but these men would have been hardened. This wasn't their first dive so they shouldn't have been disturbed by natural properties of light in water. The next expedition in 1989 had problems with its remotely operated vehicle, or ROV. Twice it lost power on a dive and both times diagnostics turned up nothing wrong with the equipment. In 1995 it was decided to raise the *Edmund*

*Fitzgerald's* bell and the HMCS *Cormorant* was dispatched to recover it. As the ship was arriving on site, its own bell crashed to the floor in the wardroom, even though the seas were not heavy at the time, and in fact, the bell had weathered much heavier seas quite often without incident. The coincidence sealed the legend of the *Edmund Fitzgerald*, and some sailors swear they have seen her sailing around Whitefish Point in the fog, eternally reliving her last voyage.

## Lake Michigan

Michigan is the third largest of the Great Lakes and is called the American Lake because it is the only one of the five Great Lakes to lie entirely within the United States.

Bordered by Michigan, Wisconsin, Illinois, and Indiana, it is 494 kilometres long and has a maximum width of 295 kilometres. The maximum depth is 282 metres and it has a drainage area of 113,750 square kilometres. Very few rivers of appreciable size drain into the lake, and one of the ones that did, the Chicago River, was reversed in 1900 so that it drains out of the lake.

The first European to see the lake was French Explorer Jean Nicolet. In 1634 the mapping of Michigan began in 1673, and the first commercial ship sailed, and sank, in 1679. The name Michigan comes from the Algonquin michigami, or misschiganin, meaning big lake.

# The Alpena

The loss of this side-wheel steamer, or paddle ship, has given its name to the storm that killed her. The Alpena storm was a sudden and unforeseen terror for many ships on the night of October 16, 1880. The previous day had been a wonderful example of Indian summer, so the drastic drop in temperature and vicious rise in winds came as a total surprise for the *Alpena* and ninety-four other vessels that night. Many did not make it to shore, including the *Alpena*. She disappeared, along with all eighty of her passengers, somewhere in southern Lake Michigan en route to Chicago. However, some people believe she still sails the lake to this day, vainly trying to make it to port. It is said that she can be seen fully lit on foggy nights, with the sounds of workers and passengers floating across the waves as she passes on her way to eternity.

# William Sanderson

There are a few stories of a *Mary Celeste*-like ship found abandoned in the Great Lakes. The *William Sanderson* made its fateful voyage just two years after the original. Unlike the *Mary Celeste*, the *William Sanderson* wasn't found abandoned on the water — she drifted ashore. She was loaded with 19,500 bushels of wheat and came ashore near Empire, Michigan. Naturally local people speculated as to the reason for the crew's disappearance. Many believed the ship must have been caught in a storm, causing the crew to panic and leave the vessel. Whatever the reason, the *William Sanderson* goes down as one of the more mysterious ships that ever sailed the Great Lakes.

## The Jamestown

Another legend of Lake Michigan is the *Jamestown*. It has been rather hard to pin down the facts, but all the ships mentioned in the legend have existed, so perhaps there is a grain of truth somewhere.

The events commonly reported in the legend took place during the American Civil War in 1862. The war was going badly for the Northern states and many believed it would only be a matter of time before the Confederate States of America would win on the battlefield, or close enough to get European recognition of their independence.

Abraham Lincoln was considered to be a one-term president, sure to lose in the 1864 election. But expectations are not reality, and this was a lesson learned by the Confederates as well as the crew of the *Flying Cloud*. They were serving on the wheat carrier late in the summer of 1862 when their ship was becalmed near Alpena. Around ten o'clock that night they were almost run down by a schooner running without lights.

This was doubly suspicious because the wind was said to be so light that it should have moved no ship, let alone a schooner. The mysterious schooner lost her wind after passing the *Flying Cloud*, though, so some of the crew rowed over and boarded her. There was no one aboard! She was deathly silent with no sign of her crew or what could have happened to them. The ship was in good order, in no sign of sinking, so there appeared to be no logical reason for her to have been abandoned. All the crew's belongings were in order, and the ship's fittings were set properly as they would be on any ordinary cruise.

The only thing out of the ordinary was that the ship's yawl was missing and the tackles were pulled up as if by a crew member on board. If the ship had been hastily abandoned via the yawl then they would still be hanging along the side of the ship.

The ship was recognized as being the *Jamestown* with a complement of nine souls. It was decided to tow her into port, so a line was strung between the two ships and a course set for port. Normally a token crew would have remained aboard the prize but in this case no one of the *Flying Cloud* would do the duty. It was probably a good thing.

Later that night a squall came up and the two ships were parted by the waves. The *Jamestown*, with her set sails, neat belongings and mysterious vanishings, was never seen again.

## The Chicora

This next ghost ship seen in Lake Michigan is said to foretell storms. The *Chicora* was built in 1892 and was sixty-seven metres long. She dependably ran passengers and freight for three years until January of 1895, when she was lost in a severe storm on the way to St. Joseph from Milwaukee.

An interesting incident occurred after her loss. For quite some time it was believed that perhaps she had made it to another port, or had run aground and would be found in time. A report came out of Chicago a month after her loss, stating she was sighted locked in the ice eleven kilometres off Chicago. Reports even came in that most of the passengers had been saved and could be seen waving their hats trying to get a passing ship's attention. However, whatever it was that these people saw, it wasn't the *Chicora*. Although bodies were never discovered, wreckage was found about fifty-seven kilometres miles north of St. Joseph and about a year later a skeletal hand was found and a cap with the letters G&M. There would be no rescue for the *Chicora* and her passengers.

The *Chicora* lives on in legend, though, especially to the many car ferries on the lake. They report seeing her off either bow for a few moments before she quickly vanishes. As the ferries' crew members predict, a severe storm follows any sighting of the ghost ship.

## Manitou Islands

These two islands are about four miles apart and are known as South Manitou Island and North Manitou Island respectively. They are forested and hilly, around six kilometres in length, and sit astride one of the busiest shipping

114

routes in Lake Michigan. They are also some of the most haunted islands anywhere. Countless people have met their fate either on or near the islands. The infamous Manitou Passage has claimed many a ship and not a few lives and some say you can still hear the desperate cries of the drowning souls from time to time. Most wreck sites are known, but some have never been found and are said to have disappeared into a crack in the lake! One of the wrecks, that of the *Francisco Morazon*, can still be seen rusted and forlorn on South Manitou Island, and it is said the ghost of a young boy who drowned can be seen near the wreck. This story has gained wide currency, so much so that park rangers are sometimes inundated with sightings.

Other stories have come down to us over the years. In the middle 1800s the islands were often used to shelter from fierce storms or for replenishment. However, they were also used to bury the dead from passing ships whose human cargo did not survive the long trip. It is suspected that some unlucky passengers who were severely ill but not dead yet were also buried here. Their wraiths are said to wander lonely stretches of coastline crying out for justice or a way home.

The islands are well covered by lighthouses, light stations, and lifesaving stations, and it seems each of them still harbours signs of their former residents. National Park personnel report loud footsteps, mysterious noises, and voices from unseen people echoing through the old structures. Lifesaving personnel were a dedicated crew and it appears that that dedication still extends into the after life.

# The Wendigo (Great Lakes, Ontario, Quebec, Arctic)

One of the more terrifying spectres said to haunt the shores of the Great Lakes comes to us from the many Native tribes that inhabit the region. To them it is known as the "evil spirit that devours mankind." This ghoul who feasts on the living is condemned to this existence through its own actions. Wendigos are originally human, but when a human resorts to cannibalism it is transformed into something hellish that walks the earth with an undying hunger for the taste of human flesh. Once this unspeakable act is performed, an evil spirit that lives in the woods waiting for this moment enters the human cannibal and takes control of the poor soul. This possession causes the human to begin uncontrollable vomiting until they die in a pool of their own blood. It is shortly after this that they are revived in the form of a monster. They are terrifying to behold; their human origins are not quite hidden by a sallow skin, glowing green eyes, yellow fangs, blue tongue, and blood-dripping lips. They are impervious to the weather and prefer to walk the night during a major snow or rainstorm when their approach is masked by the elements.

Though mainly confined to the Great Lakes area, tales of the Wendigo are also known to the Inuit of the North, as well as the Cree in Quebec. Near Lac Chibougamou in Quebec lives a Wendigo which prefers the flesh of children, especially obese specimens that cannot move quickly enough out of the path of danger. Others live

116

near Lake Memeigwess and Wendigo Lake in northern Ontario, Wendigo River in Quebec, and along the shores of the far north.

There have been especially hearty and brave native warriors who have made it their life's work to track down and slay the Wendigo. This is a difficult task since the Wendigo know every stream, cave, river, lake, and hiding place in their hunting grounds. Some have been successful, while others have fallen prey to this, the ultimate evil spirit that roams the forests and waterways of Canada.

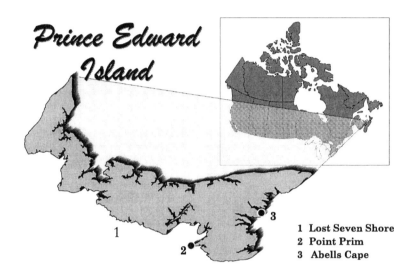

*Prince Edward Island*

1  Lost Seven Shore
2  Point Prim
3  Abells Cape

# Prince Edward Island

## Lost Seven Shore

There are not many details about the phantom ship seen here on the southern coast of Prince Edward Island, but this one stands out from the rest in the region. The ship is described as being larger than most and travels at an incredible speed, burning furiously. It is said to foretell especially severe storms that will soon hit the area.

# Point Prim

Buried treasure brings us to Point Prim, which lies along the Northumberland Strait on the southern shore of Prince Edward Island. It's not the fabled Captain Kidd Treasure, but that of the Acadians. In 1752 the British colonial authorities were worried about the many French settlers throughout Nova Scotia, New Brunswick, and Prince Edward Island. Although French, the Acadians were more often neutral in the never-ending wars between France and England. To consolidate their power, the British decided to expel all French settlers from their lands. Many ended up in Louisiana, thus the word Cajun. Some, though, made it back to the Maritimes and managed to rebuild their lives.

There are a great many legends concerning the Acadian treasure and where it was buried. Many small farmers would have buried their valuables with the hope of one day coming back to retrieve them, and there are later stories of strangers passing through and requesting lodging for the night from one of the English farmers. The next day the farmer would discover his guest had vanished and there was now a large hole nearby from which something was carried away. It is impossible to determine how much may have been hidden and eventually recovered, but local legend speaks of the ghost of an old hunchbacked Acadian man in search of his valuables. He carries a homemade shovel, and it is said he buried his treasure beside a lone pine tree before being taken away. He must have never made it back during his lifetime, for his apparition is seen walking the shore looking for the pine tree that will spell the end of his search.

## Abel's Cape

Abel's Cape in Prince Edward Island has the distinction of having a curious mixture of legends, both true and false. The most famous legend, and the most false, is that of the returning coffin. The story is that of a famous thespian, Charles Francis Coughlan, who was born in PEI and died in Galveston, Texas, in 1899. When a hurricane hit Galveston in September of 1900, it washed a great many bodies out of their graves and into the Gulf of Mexico. Consequently, because of the Gulf Stream, the coffin was carried along by the current and landed ashore near his old home.

There is an even wilder variant on this theme in the story of a Mr. Haskell, also born in PEI, who died in California and was buried there, only to be disinterred by an earthquake and carried home. The Coughlan story was a creation of Robert Ripley of *Ripley's Believe It Or Not* and both stories are related to the true story of Charles Flockton who died in California in 1904, was cremated and his ashes later interred at Abel's Cape. The Coughlan story is a staple of writers in the paranormal, but like the story of the vanishing tribe of Eskimos at Churchill Point in Manitoba, undeniably false.

As for the "true" stories connected with Abel's Cape, they concern yet another legend of Captain Kidd and his gold (he was never anywhere near the Maritimes). Phantom dogs are said to guard the burial site of immense gold and silver, somewhere along the shore of the Cape. Also seen along the shore is the ghost of a man called Abel who was murdered in 1819 and is said to roam the area groaning in agony.

1 Lac Memphrémagog
2 Lac Champlain
3 Lac Pohénégamak
4 Rivière Saguenay
5 Iles Harrington
6 Iles d'Orleans

# Quebec

## Lac Memphrémagog

Much like Lake Champlain, Lac Memprémagog both crosses the Quebec-Vermont border and has an unusual resident. But this resident is seen as being a friendly mascot rather than a mysterious creature to be feared or loathed.

Lac Memphrémagog has parallels to another lake, the fabled Loch Ness. Both are about forty kilometres long and two kilometres wide. They are around the same depth, 213 metres, and both run on a north-south axis. The creatures that inhabit the lakes are said to be of the same size and description — long, serpentine and dark. Memphré, as the local creature is called, has been seen by more than a hundred people in the last two hundred years. It is so well thought of that the cities of Magog, Quebec, and Newport, Vermont, have banded together to press for the recognition of Memphré and have called for a scientific investigation.

## Lake Champlain

Lake Champlain is over 1,130 square kilometres in size and lies mostly along the Vermont-New York State border, although it does enter into Quebec, and is connected to the St. Lawrence River via the Riviere Richelieu. It is 201 kilometres long and twenty-one kilometres wide, with an average depth of 122 metres. And it has the second most famous lake monster of North America.

Champ, as the creature is called, is like most other lake creatures in that it has the stereotypical long body, of about twelve metres in length, as well as the horse-like head and long neck. Like the others, its colour is usually dark and the body slimy. No scales have been observed, but its eyes are said to glow a bright green. The first reported European to see Champ is said to be Samuel de Champlain, but he had his sighting of a denizen of the deep in the St. Lawrence River, not Lake Champlain. The local Native tribes did see the monster often, and called him *Chaousarou,* which seems like a far more poetic name for the creature.

# Lac Pohénégamook

Another fiercer monster is said to inhabit this lake, and goes by the name of Ponik. The first sign of his presence is a large foamy wake as he moves through the water. He is said to have a mane down his neck and a sawtooth back, which is a rarity among lake monster traditions, although it has been seen in Sweden and British Columbia. Some believe the sawtooth back is a sign of masculinity and that Ponik's mate would have less clearly defined ridges. Ponik has large pectoral and ventral fins and its colour is described as darkish gray or black, with a horse-like head. The fierce nature of Ponik comes not from any behavioural study, but because of the way it looks. Ponik has been studied by the Quebec Ministry of Fish and Game, and they believe the monster is actually a sturgeon. Sturgeons do have a prehistoric look about them, but this doesn't explain the horse-like head nor large foamy wake the creature leaves behind. The actual nature of the creature remains a mystery.

# Gatineau Hills

The Gatineau Hills have been a refuge for citizens of Ottawa, particularly politicians and Prime Ministers, for many years. But the area north of the National Capital Region is also known for its tales of mysterious creatures that are said to inhabit nine interconnected lakes. The lakes include

Desert, Blue Sea, Baskatong, Cedar, St. Clair, Pocknock, Bitobo, Tortue, and Trente et Un Milles. The creatures said to inhabit these lakes are long, dark, and horse-headed, with serpentine bodies, and manes down their necks. They are believed to be the strongest of all lake monsters since they leave the fiercest wakes behind them as they move along the lakes and the rivers between them. They are commonly called the Blue Sea Monsters, since it is from that lake that the most reports originate. They undulate across the lakes, but only in warmer weather, never being seen in winter. They are believed to be shy retiring creatures with a curiosity for humans. Like most lake monsters, these are seen as favourite pets rather than frightening visions by local residents.

## Saguenay River

In 1535 when Jacques Cartier returned a second time to present day Quebec, the Natives he met spun him a tale that captured his imagination. They spoke of this fabulous kingdom that was rich in gold and jewels, just waiting for the taking. They were rather vague as to its location, but the Saguenay River was the road to riches, and thus Cartier set out to find this mythical land.

Other tribes told other explorers similar stories of this mythical kingdom. Depending on the teller, the kingdom could be anywhere from the headwaters of the Saguenay River to Lake Superior. The residents of this land spoke a Latin-like language and the capital was called Sagana. Even the king of France was taken in by this tall tale, and thus in some small way, the Natives exacted a form of revenge on the many people who walked over their lives in the greedy pursuit of gold and treasure.

## Iles Harrington

Scholars believe it is one of these islands that so terrified explorers in the sixteenth century. They are a dark and gloomy spot, thought of by many as one of the most desolate places on earth. They are also thought to be the legendary Iles des Demons. Jacques Cartier recounted stories of the islands being haunted by devils.

In 1541 Jean François de La Rocque de Roberval was appointed Lieutenant-Governor of New France. On his voyage to the New World, he noticed his niece, Marguerite, consorting with a member of the crew with whom she was having a passionate love affair. Being of a cruel heart, Roberval set his niece and a serving girl on an uninhabited island then called Iles des Demons. They did have firearms and foodstuffs, but their life expectancy was limited, needless to say. Her lover, upon hearing of the cruel decision of Roberval, jumped ship and joined his love on their lonely island.

Poor Marguerite did survive her torment, although her lover, the servant girl, and a child all died in the three years before her rescue. She was one of the few who survived this desolate and haunting place. To this day the Iles Harrington evoke fear in those sailors or fishermen who pass by them, muttering a silent prayer to escape the torment of Marguerite or the power of the devil.

## Ile d'Orleans

A French sorcerer named Jean-Pierre Lavallee is said to haunt this island that is near Quebec City. His spirit still walks the island protecting it from intruders. In 1711 the British sailed up the St. Lawrence River with the intention of attacking Quebec City. Lavallee had the unique power to control weather so he called down a thick fog to obscure the enemy fleet and make any attempt to navigate farther towards Quebec impossible. The English retreated and Lavallee's reputation was assured.

But Lavallee is not the only spirit to haunt this historic island. There are many other phantoms to be found here — unfortunate sailors who have died on or near the island over the years and who cannot leave this earthly realm. Some are seen in traditional human form; others manifest themselves as wandering ghost lights that move aimlessly around the island.

# Saskatchewan

1 Turtle Lake
2 Qu'Appelle River

# Saskatchewan

## Turtle Lake

Turtle Lake falls under the heading of a lake monster with few details, but because it is always mentioned in local lore, I will cover it here.

The Turtle Lake Monster, which made its debut in 1923, is said to be the most terrifying lake creature in Canada. Fiercely aggressive, this nasty beast destroys fishermen's nets and is described as having a long neck, three humps, and is variously dog-headed, pig-headed, or horse-headed. Take your pick. Some of the stories suggest sturgeon, while others remain unclassifiable.

# Qu'Appelle River

One of the prettiest and most romantic tales haunts this river. No horse-headed creatures here, just a beautiful valley with a sad tale of lost love. Qu'Appelle means "Who calls?" in French, but the original Cree name for the valley and river was *Kahtapwao* which means "What is calling?"

The story has it that a Cree man was traveling far to see his sweetheart, for they were soon to be married. He paddled his canoe for days through the beautiful valley of lakes and rivers until the night before he was to arrive to see his betrothed. He was exhausted from the trip and let his canoe be carried along by the current with no help from him. As the full moon rose over the river he was startled to hear his name called with a tender whisper. The surprised brave called out, "Who calls?" but was only answered with another whispered call of his name. He called out again, "Who calls?" but there was no answer. Fearing the worst, the brave redoubled his efforts and reached the village of his sweetheart just before sunrise. There he found the whole tribe in deep mourning for his true love.

As recounted in Jo-Anne Christensen's delightful book *Ghost Stories of Saskatchewan*, an elder woman of the tribe comforted the young man as he grieved over the young maiden's body.

"She called for you twice last night," said the woman.

Shaken, he asked when.

"As the moon was rising, just before she passed away."

132

It is said to this day you can hear the young maiden's haunting cry for her love as the moon first rises over the horizon.

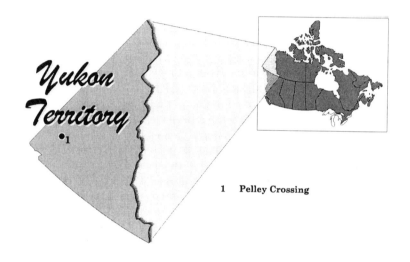

1    Pelley Crossing

# Yukon

## Near Pelly Crossing

Not all water ghosts are found in lakes, rivers, or oceans. A dense bog can harbour its own creepy manifestations, and the boggy land near Pelly Crossing spawned a story that is unique among ghost stories.

Pelly Crossing is north of Whitehorse, the capital of Yukon Territory. The surrounding countryside is barren and bleak, mostly scrub brush and a few gnarled shrubs and trees. There is also another aspect to the land that is particular to northern lands. In the Yukon it is known as muskeg. Above a certain latitude it is too cold for the land to ever thaw out. This permafrost can be found at varying levels below the surface. Every year the surface ice and snow will melt during the summer but have nowhere to go. It is trapped above the permafrost, but below the visible level of the ground. Therefore, the unwary trekker can be travelling across what appears to be flat, even ground when they are suddenly slugging through endless kilometres of mucky bog.

Into this land, which is starkly beautiful in its own way, came a man who is referred to in various reports as Jerry. Jerry was a prospector who was familiar with the area and its dangers. One particular day, however, Jerry suddenly found himself in a seemingly endless expanse of muskeg and so he took shelter on a mound of stable land with only one scraggly tree and some scrub brush for company. He was able to build a small fire while he contemplated his predicament and tried to determine the best way out of the muck. He thought long and hard about his situation until the tiredness forced his eyes closed.

His sleep was soon interrupted by the sound of voices, and they appeared to be close. Jerry's dog Max began to growl at the same time, and when he opened his eyes he was surprised to see the vision of four adult men and a teenage girl a short distance away. They were heatedly speaking to each other in a language that Jerry did not recognize but amazingly he felt he understood what they were saying. The men were angry at his presence while the younger girl was trying to calm them down. As Jerry fully roused himself and got up to meet the apparent threat the five wraiths disappeared. Not entirely believing what had just happened, Jerry sat back down and drifted off to sleep.

A short time later Max began to growl again and looking up Jerry saw his visitors had returned. Again they were abusive towards him so Jerry got up to defend himself and hurled some abusive language of his own. At this the apparitions disappeared again and Jerry, now totally confused, resumed his perch on a dry part of the mound. No sooner had he sat down than Max began to whimper and looking up, Jerry saw that the teenage girl was standing before him alone in the dark. She spoke to him kindly and explained how he could find his way out of his dangerous predicament. She then faded out and Jerry and Max found themselves alone for the rest of the night.

The next morning Jerry was a little unsure of the events of the previous night, but he decided that he had nothing to lose by following his ghostly benefactor's directions. Sure enough, he was able to find his way through the treacherous muskeg and to firmer ground. Eventually he reached his home and told others of his mysterious trip. Many of his friends refused to believe him, and indeed, the story is unlike most ghostly lore. However, author Sheila Hervey in her book *Canada Ghost to Ghost* did believe Jerry and did a little research to try to determine the possible identities of the strange wraiths in the dark arctic night. She was able to find reports of a Serbian family who passed though Fort Edmonton, Alberta, in 1874 heading for the Yukon River, and she believes the mysterious apparitions may have been this family, especially since they had a teenage daughter of the approximate age of the girl who saved a desperate prospector in his hour of need.

# The Scientific Search
## for the Truth

After many years of solitary investigation by such groups as the Society for Psychical Research and the American Society for Psychical Research, the 1990s saw an enormous increase in the number of people and organizations searching for the truth in the area of the paranormal. This has been both a blessing and a curse, for there has been a concurrent increase in false and misleading information. Without meaning to sound elitist, the lack of professionals in this field has made research and investigations very difficult. A researcher in the area of the paranormal has to be well read in a wide range of fields such as psychology, sociology, neuroscience, astronomy, biology, zoology, geology, history, photography, and theology, to name a few. Too many writers and researchers are only interested in promoting their own philosophical, pseudo-religious opinions as theories or facts. Most professional researchers have advanced university degrees.

In 1996 I founded (and serve as Executive Director of) the Center For Parapsychological Studies in Canada (CPSC) as a research organization devoted to the accumulation of reputable information and the dissemination of that knowledge to the media and public at large. Since 1998 we at the Center have also taken on an investigative role, primarily in the areas of hauntings and ESP (psychics). We gather current information on reputable schools in parapsychology, research organizations around the world, and theories to explain some of the more interesting areas of the paranormal. We are always looking to hear from people who have experienced a strange event or want to learn where to look for more information. Our website should answer most of your questions but feel free to contact us at any time. My own personal website gives a little more biographical information as well as my upcoming writing projects, and I am always looking to hear from anyone who just wants to tell a good story.

Thank you for your interest in this book.

The Center For Parapsychological Studies in Canada
P.O. Box 29091
7001 Mumford Rd
Halifax, Nova Scotia, Canada B3L 4T8
1-902-453-1905
www.cpsc.cjb.net or www.cpscghosts.com


Darryll Walsh
6533 Edgewood Avenue
Halifax, Nova Scotia, Canada B3L 2P1
1-902-453-1905
novajodik@hfx.andara.com
www.darryllwalsh.cjb.net

# Bibliography

Baigent, Michael, and Richard Leigh, and Henry Lincoln. *The Holy Blood and the Holy Grail* London: Jonathan Cape, 1982.

Boyer, Dwight. *Ghost Ships of the Great Lakes.* New York: Dodd, Mead and Co., 1968.

Bradley, Michael. *Holy Grail Across the Atlantic: The Secret History of Canadian Discovery and Exploration.* Willowdale, Ontario: Hounslow Press, 1988.

Bercusion, David J., and J.L. Granatstein. *The Collins Dictionary of Canadian History: 1867-Present.* Toronto: Collins, 1988.

Blackman, W. Haden. *The Field Guide to North American Hauntings*. New York: Three Rivers Press, 1998.

Blackman, W. Haden. *The Field Guide to North American Monsters*. New York: Three Rivers Press, 1998.

Campbell, Lyall. *Sable Island: Fatal and Fertile Crescent*. Hantsport, NS: Lancelot Press, 1990.

Christensen, Jo-Anne. *Ghost Stories of Saskatchewan*. Toronto: Hounslow Press, 1995.

Coleman, Loren and Clark, Jerome. *Cryptozoology A-Z: The Encyclopedia of Loch Monsters, Sasquatch, Chupacabras, and Other Authentic Mysteries of Nature*. New York: A Fireside Book (Simon & Schuster), 1999.

Colombo, John Robert. *Mysterious Canada: Strange Sights, Extraordinary Events, and Peculiar Places*. Toronto: Doubleday Canada, 1988.

Creighton, Helen. *Bluenose Ghosts*. Toronto: McGraw-Hill Ryerson, 1957.

Crooker, William S. *Oak Island Gold*. Halifax, NS: Nimbus Publishing Ltd, 1993.

Editors of Reader's Digest. *Reader's Digest Atlas of Canada*. Toronto: The Reader's Digest Association (Canada) Ltd, 1995.

Finan, Mark. *Oak Island Secrets*. Halifax, NS: Formac Publishing, 1995.

Furneaux, Rupert. *Money Pit: The Mystery of Oak Island*. Toronto: Totem Books, 1972.

Gaddis, Vincent. *Invisible Horizons: True Mysteries of the Sea*. New York: Chilton Book Company, 1965.

Harris, Graham, and Les MacPhie. *Oak Island and Its Lost Treasure*. Halifax, NS: Formac Publishing, 2000.

Hauck, Dennis William. *Haunted Places. The National Directory: Ghostly Abodes, Sacred Sites, UFO Landings and Other Supernatural Locations*. New York: Penguin Books, 1996.

Hervey, Sheila. *Canada Ghost to Ghost*. Toronto: Stoddart Publishing, 1996.

Hervey, Sheila. *Some Canadian Ghosts*. Toronto: Pocket Books, 1973.

Kirk, John. *In the Domain of the Lake Monsters*. Toronto: Key Porter Books Ltd, 1988

Sherwood, Roland. *The Phantom Ship of Northumberland Strait and Other Mysteries of the Sea*. Hantsport, NS: Lancelot Press, 1975.

Smith, Barbara. *Ghost Stories of Alberta*. Toronto: Hounslow Press, 1993.

Sonin, Eileen. *More Canadian Ghosts.* Toronto: Pocket Books, 1974.

Spaeth, Frank, Ed. *Mysteries of the Deep: Amazing Phenomena in our World's Waterways.* St. Paul, Minnesota: Llewellyn Publications, 1998.

Stonehouse, Frederick. *Haunted Lakes: Great Lake Ghost Stories, Superstitions and Sea Serpents.* Duluth, Minnesota: Lake Superior Port Cities Inc., 1997.

Trueman, Stuart. *Ghosts, Pirates, and Treasure Trove: The Phantoms That Haunt New Brunswick.* Toronto: McClelland and Stewart Ltd, 1975.

Walsh, Darryll. *Ghosts of Nova Scotia.* Halifax, Nova Scotia: Pottersfield Press, 2000.